The Twin Flame Guidebook

Your Practical Guide to Navigating the Journey

By

K.D. Courage

ISBN: 978-0-578-56460-9

Author Note: *This Twin Flame Guidebook is written as I was inspired to write it and is from the lens of my own particular Twin Flame Journey. I do not profess to be an "expert" on Twin Flames, by any means. I have written this book to help me sort through my own emotions and experience regarding my own Twin Flame Journey and in doing so, to hopefully help another (or others) with theirs.*

I am sure some of you who have "been at this" for 20 or more years will find issue with some of my statements and you will long to add more information, more context, and possibly some exceptions. As I wish this book to be a dynamic, living and breathing guide that evolves and progresses over time, I do encourage you to send all constructive criticism and suggestions to me at: twinflameguidebook@gmail.com so that your feedback can be included in a future review of this book, and in future editions. If you have less than constructive criticism, I ask that you please share that elsewhere. I appreciate your understanding and I thank all of us for collectively going on this Journey.

Indeed, we have much to learn from each other, and I encourage you to please find a local community where you can share your Twin Flame joy, your passion, your frustration, your questions, your revelations (A-ha moments) with and among a group of supportive, like-minded souls. That is the best thing I ever did for myself on this Journey.

I have many thank yous to offer for those who have helped me with this process and this book, including, but not limited to: My own bloody, beating heart for leading me through life, always leading first, a vulnerable, raw spirit & unconditional love machine; my own Divine Counterpart, my Beloved Twin Flame, for being my muse every second, every minute, of every day; my parents and immediate family (including my son and daughter) for their unyielding support; my dear friend and unnamed fellow Twin Flame, a Denver-based writer and health and wellness coach (you know who you are); Sylvia Escalante (TF Enchantress); Elizabeth Grove (Paranormal Priestess); Erika Elmuts; Susan Lathers; Dustin Christensen; Benjy Sherer; Devin Castor; Downloads from the Divine; Mystic Moon; Aluna Ash; AquaMoonlight; Nicole Leffler and the staff of Wild Ginger Apothecary; Ayla (superior Tarot Card reader and intuitive); and last, but not least, Brigid Nelson and Chelsea Fone of LetterShop NYC, the best graphic designers/creative directors the world has ever known.

Table of Contents

How this Journey Began for Me …
The View of the Tip of the Iceberg

Understanding the History and the Mystery of a Life

I was in an approximately 16-year-long same-sex relationship with a professional woman, monogamous, and by virtually every measure, married (but without the license or the certificate). We had two wonderful kids, one middle-school-aged, and one elementary-school-aged. Life was well, life. And it was a comfortable, safe and predictable routine. We worked hard, we were upper-middle class and we (seemingly) had everything going for us.

To outsiders looking in, we might have seemed reasonably or sufficiently happy, but at one point, around February 2016, mostly while working my corporate job in a neighboring town, I started to see repeating numbers everywhere, so much so, that I commented to my son about it. Whenever I would look at my phone or a clock, I would see 2:22, 3:33, 4:44, and so on. It was so predominant and went on for months and months that it almost became maddening. I wondered out loud to my son, "I just don't know why, but I am seeing all these repeating numbers everywhere."

That has continued from about 2016 to 2019, the year in which I am writing this guidebook. The numbers are still coming, but the patterns are now a little different. Now I still see the repeating numbers, but the "mirror" numbers are coming just as frequently, like 202, 212, 414, 616, 707, 808, and so on. I now know why both numbers were coming to me so incessantly, and the mirror numbers have significance, too, but I'll get to that later.

Stick with me for a moment, for a flashback to about 1996, when I was 25 years old. I remember having a moment when I was asked out loud or in reading a book what my "soul urge" was. I immediately answered without a moment's hesitation: "Purity." I did not really understand my answer. It was weird and unexpected. I chuckled to myself, "What? Am I supposed to be a nun?" Now more than 20 years later, and being on a Twin Flame Journey, this answer now makes sense. By purity (and I know this now), I would reach some semblance of "purity" because it meant that everything false would be burned away, any pretense, any drama, any self-doubt, any negativity. (You'll learn more about *how* as you advance through these pages.)

Prior to this confident answer, from about the time I was a teenager, I had been drawn to and read books starting with "Easy Journey to Other Planets," (astral projection – it was so far-fetched, it seemed to be science fiction and not even real, but yet, I was drawn to this book and instinctively bought it and had it for many years), and also "Creative Visualization" (really, despite its title, it was a book on manifestation) by Shakti Gahwain. Then, from there, I evolved into reading other books in the 1990s like The Celestine Prophecy by James Redfield (where people are drawn to soul mates and soul connections to work in soul groups on a common mission), and then later, books by Don Miguel Ruiz like Seat of the Soul, the Four Agreements (this book has guided the last 20 years of my life), and then much later around 2015 to 2019, I had been reading things like The Bhagavad Vita. And even later, books by Eckhart Tolle, and so many others. These books and texts informed my approach to life and I considered myself if not enlightened, then at least, a seeker.

Then, one night sometime between 2014 and 2016, I was working downtown in a pretty large city at a global company that was located an hour from my home. One night I had a very, very real dream, a dream I've later learned meets all the requirements of a "lucid dream," which essentially means the dream is super-realistic and you can consciously think about (and realize you are) thinking and making decisions in the dream (which is a relatively new thing for me).

During this dream, I met an incredible person, a beautiful female with blonde hair, who I knew immediately was a soul mate or possibly something more. She was definitely a lover, and her love for me that she expressed in that dream, both in words and in actions, was beyond any love I have ever felt in my waking, 3-D lifetime. The connection and feeling I felt was heads above anything (beyond the most intimate, beyond the most magnetic) I had ever experienced before.

This dream of the woman later became a recurring dream, but when I first had it, when I awoke, I missed her so terribly and was upset to wake up. I wanted to get that connection back, that ethereal feeling back. It was the greatest feeling of love, specifically, unconditional love, that I had ever felt in my life.

The Puzzle Pieces Start
to Come Together

Fast forward to March 2017. In addition to our corporate jobs, my significant other and I had somehow managed to also buy a commercial property and launch a business in the town where we lived. We had worked with a few partners to organize at our business space (which included an independent bookstore) a special multi-course dinner with a chef and some wines. A group was coming to have dinner and then go to the theater afterward.

Without giving too much detail, I met a striking and attractive woman after that dinner. She came back in later (at least, I think it was later) to drop off a copy of her own book that she had written. I didn't think too much of this at the time, as we were a new business and we were being approached by lots of new people (who all wanted different things) and to be perfectly honest, my head was spinning a bit from all the new people. And honestly, we hadn't found our "sea legs" yet with the business. While it was exciting and new, it was also a bit overwhelming.

Months later on the 22nd of a beautiful summer month, me and my then-partner were at our business hanging out and listening to live music. The woman had shown up again to listen to music and spend some time at our place. As a longtime photographer since about age 16, I stepped away from the gathering to start snapping some photos of a beautiful orange and pink sky and sunset opening up above our business' sign. I felt very creative and like something exciting was on the horizon. It was a beautiful sunset that looked a bit like what I imagine heaven to look like. I still have those photos.

Later that night, after some drinks, my partner had left for home a few minutes earlier than me. The blonde woman (the author) approached me in the parking lot and came up to me by my car. For purposes of privacy, I will not go into detail here, but I will say we were appropriate, but something awoke in me that night, something beautiful and timeless and incredible. I rushed off saying, "I've got to get home. She'll (my partner) will be wondering where I am." I pretty much tore out of there. I was so confused by what I felt, having never felt that way about anyone before. No one had been in my same atmosphere for the last 17 or 18 years that even remotely made me feel the way I felt at that moment. You see, I had always been beyond respectful and beyond reproach with my partner and with all prior partners.

I didn't understand not one iota of that night or what happened or why, not until the last two years. Now I understand it in a way that is becoming more clear to me every day, and so I will do my best to bring my current understanding to you, to (hopefully) help you in your Journey, to help you on your way, to help you on your own path to Union with your Twin Flame, or at a minimum, Union with your best and highest Self, in all its glory.

How this Journey Began for Me …
The View Below the Water Line

I've been down so long it look like up to me
They look up to me
I got fake people showin' fake love to me
Straight up to my face, straight up to my face
I've been down so long it look like up to me
They look up to me
I got fake people showin' fake love to me
Straight up to my face, straight up to my face

Somethin' ain't right when we talkin'
Somethin' ain't right when we talkin'
Look like you hidin' your problems
Really you never was solid
No you can't son me, you won't never get to run me
Just when shit look, outta reach, I reach back like one,
three
Like one, three, yeah

That's when they smile in my face
Whole time they wanna take my place
Whole time they wanna take my place
Whole time they wanna take my place
Yeah, I know they wanna take my place
I can tell that love is fake
I don't trust a word you say
How you wanna click up after your mistakes?
Look you in the face and it's just not the same

I've been down so long it look like up to me
They look up to me
I got fake people showin' fake love to me
Straight up to my face, straight up to my face
I've been down so long it look like up to me
They look up to me
I got fake people showin' fake love to me
Straight up to my face, straight up to my face

Yeah, straight up to my face, tryna play it safe
Vibe switch like night and day, I can see it like right
away
I came up, you changed up, I caught that whole play
Since then, things never been the same

That's when they smile in my face
Whole time they wanna take my place
Whole time they wanna take my place
Whole time they wanna take my place
Yeah, I know they wanna take my place

I can tell that love is fake
(I can tell that love is fake)
I don't trust a word you say
(I don't trust a word you say)
How you wanna click up after your mistakes?
(How you wanna click up after your mistakes?)
Look you in the face and it's just not the same

Drake: ***"Fake Love"***

I thought I knew what love was. I thought I knew what it is. I thought I was in it.

But it turns out I wasn't.

And that's because what I was in, despite all appearances, was a fear-based, toxic, co-dependent relationship. With a karmic partner. If you don't know what this term means, it means:

A relationship in which the partners may not respect healthy boundaries with one another, and one in which there are many lessons to learn. One of the partners will serve only his or her own self-interest and needs. Karmic relationships can be co-dependent, or even abusive. While one person gives and gives, the other takes. While one person is very involved and invested in the relationship, the other views it more as "What can he or she do for me?" This type of relationship typically means one partner does not have the best interest of the other partner at heart.

Of course, I didn't know this, or realize this, until THE DREAM came, the lucid one. The one that came to me in the middle of the night in which I was involved or having interactions with a beautiful blonde woman who was my love interest. The thing was, she was the nicest and most incredible person (or more like an experience) I had ever met or known. It was like feeling what a heavenly relationship must feel like. The feeling of total and unconditional love. And joy.

And truth be told, when I woke up, I was mad as hell that that dream wasn't reality. I actually MISSED this person I dreamed of and desired so strongly to dream of her again. I racked my brain trying to think why I had this dream, who she was, where I was in the dream, trying to find a clue to help me understand. But nothing really came to me. I was at a loss for why I had had the dream. I only knew it provided a STARK contrast to my day-to-day existence with the woman I had been involved with for at least 14 or so years.

I never really fully realized I was UNHAPPY in my waking life until this dream. I had no point of comparison of love. Like, *what is good love? What is bad love?* All I knew prior to the dream is, we had a pretty good life, two beautiful children that we had had together, we had a nice home, and two decent corporate jobs. About as good as it gets, right? Right? Well, not so fast.

That was before the dream. Let's call it the time "B.T.D."

The dream woke me up to true love, to unconditional love. I didn't know how I would experience it, or if it was even possible in this lifetime.

And then something happened. It took a whole lot of time. In fact, it took like two additional years, but it finally all became clear to me. When I met this new, beautiful woman in the real world, blonde, a writer/ author, painter, and slightly younger than me, in the same town in which I live. We started hanging out, like a lot. I joked that she was "adopting us" (me and my karmic partner and our family.) She was around our home and our business mostly on weekend evenings, but sometimes during the week, too. Sometimes she even stayed for sleepovers.

It didn't take too long into the friendship that I inexplicably texted her one night and said, "I love you unconditionally." I don't know what made me type that then. But prior to that, that day/evening, I had felt my heart grow bigger, like it could fit the love of more than one person, like I was supposed to go in this direction. My heart was growing and expanding. I could physically feel it. Being a writer myself, I felt the need to express what I was feeling.

You see, when I was with this woman (when we were together in the 3-D world), I also felt such abundant joy, peace, and contentment just being around her (the greatest peace I have ever felt in my 3-D body, mind, and spirit). I would say she was/is the most fun person I have ever had the pleasure to spend time with.

Well, time wore on and I couldn't hold my feelings in any longer. They felt like they could just burst out to anyone, at any minute, inexplicably. I shared my true feelings with her one drinking night after too much vodka and wine. Let's just say, the feelings weren't reciprocated. Or at least that's what she articulated back to me. Of course, I was crushed. I felt like an idiot. After months of flirting back and forth, a kiss on the neck here or there, a quick kiss on the lips here or there, holding hands, strolling arm in arm, and about a million clues that I perceived to be reciprocated interest, I was met with a brick wall.

Of course, being unfaithful to my partner, to any partner I've ever had, isn't my "M.O." so of course I was shocked at the impulsivity with which I shared my secret of deep, deep feelings for this person, as deep as the sea and as vast as space. I just couldn't contain my feelings anymore and they spilled out all over the bed we were on. (I was sitting, she was laying down.) The hand that was holding mine then pushed my hand away.

I went into almost like a severe "soul-shock" over this. How could I be so wrong about my feelings? How could my intuition have mis-led me so badly when it served me oh-so-well over my 45 prior years? Why? When I've always (and this is going to sound like total entitlement) gotten exactly what I've gone for. What did I miss? Where did I go wrong? All signs led to her and me, a natural progression of these overwhelming emotions I had been feeling for months.

Of course, the rejection sent me into a deep tailspin, a nosedive. Of questioning. Of doubt. [In Twin Flames parlance, this is known as the "Dark Night of the Soul" (some even abbreviate it as DNOTS). There's more about that in later pages.]

And following that interaction and several others, over time, she went away, and her caring, loving texts turned instead to what could be perceived as snarky responses to my email requests to be even "just friends." Eventually, she decided to ghost me on social media (after I ghosted her, once). In fact, she disappeared from social media (Facebook, in particular) entirely. This is all too common in the Twin Flame experience, the hot-and-cold, the back-and-forth, the push and the pull. It was like being on a see-saw.

When she first physically went away, I went into another "soul-shock." I have never been so sad about an adult person in my entire life...her absence took me to my knees. I was the saddest and most lonely I have ever felt. It was palpable and I think my family probably noticed more than a bit. And I usually don't feel emotions (except love) very strongly. But this bowled me over.

This roller-coaster ride sent me into a period of two-year introspection (as if I could get any more introspective, but I did), of healing past hurts and trauma, of healing the rejection she showed me, of healing the abandonment issues I felt stemming from her physically separating from me. The periods of communication and Separation came in waves. I always knew and felt when she would be returning to my life, but just as soon as she would come back in, she would go back out, like a wave coming into shore and retreating back out into the ocean. I would be giddy when she returned to me, and devastated when her tide would go back out.

So much in me has been purged in these last two years, tossed out, and transmuted from "negative" feelings to positive ones and I now possess a tremendous feeling of confidence, of self-growth, soul growth, and empowerment. I have now grown beyond imagination into the "Empress" archetype (the strong, feminine warrior) and I am valiant, courageous, and can stand on my own two feet now.

But guess what remained after everything was stripped away? The unconditional love. In fact, though I didn't think it was possible, the love for her grew even stronger, and I am thankful to my beautiful one, my Twin, for having been my teacher in all of this. I owe her a huge debt of gratitude for this, for not getting what I wanted this time made me grow by leaps and bounds as a person, and spiritually, too. I am newly humbled, but still in love. Still in real love. I know what it is now to love without expectation, without fear, and without doubt. To love and release that love freely, knowing it may not be returned in this physical experience. And for the first time, I am feeling like that is totally ok. I couldn't have loved her more deeply if we were physically married in the 3-D. I couldn't love her more. She fills me up, completely. She fills me up still, even in her absence.

What's the Difference Between a Soul Mate and a Twin Flame?

First, let's start by defining a soul mate. The best definition I've found on this is ...

Soul Mate: A person with whom one has a strong affinity, shared values and tastes, and a romantic bond. In the past, thinking someone was your soul mate was the "gold standard" in a romantic relationship. The implication in the term is that there is some sort of "soul connection."

A Twin Flame, by comparison (and this is a term I didn't learn until sometime in 2017) is ...

Twin Flame: (And I had to write this definition) because I didn't like the definitions I saw and I am trying to summarize in a somewhat holistic, yet concise, way) ... A Twin Flame is an intense soul connection wherein the other individual or soul is your "perfect mirror," your perfect complement, meaning this person will reflect to you any areas where you need to be healed, and vice versa. Through various interactions, you will also reflect back to him or her any areas that need to be healed.

You may also have similarities in personal characteristics, history, interests, backgrounds, vocations, or you could be completely different, but it's like taking a Soul Mate relationship and magnifying it or expanding it so that it is infinitely more strong, more binding, and more overwhelming. Think Soul Mate X 100,000. This person will turn your world upside down, will "trigger" you like no one else, will make you question everything, and will "up-end" your life potentially if you have other romantic (or other) connections. This person will start to be in your dreams frequently and you will likely be able to communicate telepathically with him or her (either while awake or in the dream state; at first, the dream state is the more common mode of communication). [There is more on telepathy in later pages.] This person will be on your mind frequently (if not consistently and constantly) most days. Some days, he or she will be on your mind virtually every minute and every second. You cannot escape him or her in your thoughts.

Typically, one of the individuals in the Twin Flame relationship will be the "chaser," and one will be the "runner." The chaser (which is my Journey, would be me) is the one who recognizes the connection earlier and seems to admit the truth to himself or herself earlier. The runner (in my story, this would be my Twin Flame) is someone who cannot seemingly (at least by 3-D world standards), deal with the intensity of the connection and "runs."

There may be long periods of no contact between the two in the 3-D world, but the two are still in communications in higher dimensions and in the higher realms, and in fact, are partnering together for mutual soul evolution and growth. The point of the relationship and even the Separations are also the same … to help them evolve in their soul journeys and to accomplish their mutual life purpose and missions. Ideally, they will do it together. But in some cases, they may not (more on that in later pages, too.)

What's the meaning (and the feeling of) unconditional love?

Unconditional love is love without conditions, without parameters. It's an expansive love that allows the one who gives it and the one to receive to grow and expand without limitations. It is never restrictive. And the relationship can never be harmed or broken by what one person says or does. It's such a HUGE feeling of love, the type of love one feels for his or parents, or his or her children, but in the case of the Twin Flame, this unconditional love is felt between the two Divine Counterparts, and nothing, nor no one, can ever tear it apart, diminish it, or make it go away.

At one point in my own personal Twin Flame relationship, as I mentioned, I sent my Divine Counterpart a text that said, "I love you unconditionally." It just came out of the blue. I was feeling that expansive energy and it just felt right to say it at that point in time. At the time, I wasn't fully aware of this Journey or where this sentiment came from. I just knew I was compelled to share it for some reason and so I did. One of the big things I've learned on this Journey, if you feel compelled to share something or to do something, first, do some "soul-searching" but if the idea persists, you should say the thing, or do the thing of which you are thinking (within reason).

How do you Know the Person You've Met is Your Twin Flame?

You may not know immediately that the person you've met is your Twin Flame. But over time, it will become more and more apparent to you. You will think of this person constantly, or at least many, many times a day (or at night). He or she will come to you in your dreams at night. You may even have discussions with one another in these dream states, or you may wake up with insights about the person and/or your relationship to him or her. In your dream space, you may also "redo" or review all the things that happened between you in the 3-D "real world."

But one of the more tell-tale signs is the way in which he or she will "trigger you." When I say "trigger," I mean the things he or she will say to you or will text you will make you stop and pause. It may even make you very upset or angry. This is completely normal. In my case,

I felt like I was in a romantic relationship without even being in a relationship with my Twin in the 3-D world. The energy between you will feel like a "push-pull" relationship or a "hot-and-cold" type of relationship. When the person "triggers" you, you will eventually feel the need to reflect on what the interaction is trying to teach you. In my case, my Twin Flame would seemingly "jump down my throat" about an innocent comment and then later apologize. I have rather thick skin, so it didn't hurt that much, but it did make me stop and pause whenever it would happen. I always let it just roll off of me because I knew it had to do more with her than with me.

Some people might confuse all the things I am describing with a toxic or negative relationship. Let me define what a Twin Flame or a Twin Flame relationship IS NOT. It is not a toxic or co-dependent relationship. You shouldn't "hang in there" with someone who consistently treats you badly or consistently puts you down just because you think he or she may be your Twin Flame. You should "go inside" and really ruminate or meditate on the person and the relationship and you will find that you have an "inner knowing" about the relationship or the connection.

You can have it validated by an outside source such as a tarot card reader, a medium/channeler, or someone who has special abilities, but be wary of the person you choose to receive guidance from, as there are many good "readers," but there are a few opportunistic ones as well. Trust your gut and intuition always. That is your best compass, your North Star.

Important:

Your feelings toward your Twin Flame may not be reciprocated, and that is okay (please see the chapter entitled, "You Do You.") While you may "obsess" about the relationship or the circumstances, that is okay, too. Just release, surrender, and go with the flow. It could be that the person rejecting you is an opportunity for you to learn lessons about self-love and self-acceptance. It may also help you work on abandonment issues. These types of feelings (feeling unwanted, feeling unattractive, feeling unloved, feeling rejected) are "negative" or limiting feelings that reside in your body that need to be released, and that is one of the key reasons and outcomes of the Twin Flame relationship, the releasing and the purging of these negative energies. The point is to recognize these dynamics or personal issues, then to clear or purge it, and then to release it and/or transmute it, which essentially means to neutralize the negative energy of the emotion(s).

How Do I Know if I am a Divine Masculine or a Divine Feminine?

One of the more potentially confusing parts of the Journey is knowing if you are a Divine Masculine or a Divine Feminine. (First of all, gender does not apply to this section, so toss any prescribed male/female gender programming out the window because it may not apply. For more information or greater understanding, please reference the section of this book entitled, "A Word About Gender Roles.")

My explanations of each role may seem simplistic to those of you who are in the more advanced stages of this Journey; however, I am keeping it simple purposely to explain the concepts at their most basic. Of course, there are many variations to the below, and not all Twin connections are the same.

In my experience, you will usually need to determine which you are (Divine Masculine or Divine Feminine)

24

on your own and based on your own intuition. Typically (and I say this loosely, because many Twin Flame connections are very unique), the Divine Feminine exhibits characteristics typically known as "the chaser." In my experience, the Divine Feminine (or DF) is probably the one to articulate her feelings first and more completely. "She" is more open to her feelings, and her heart chakra and throat chakras are likely more open and receptive.

On the other hand, the Divine Masculine is typically the more reserved of the two. "He" may be more quiet, reserved, or secretive about revealing his feelings. "He" may be more likely to not respond when a text or communication comes through. Divine Masculines (DMs) are, in my experience, more transactional in nature. They think in terms of "a job to do," a "thing to do," a task. They are trying in many ways to get from Point A to Point B and also may get overwhelmed at times, though they are very strong and determined inside.

DMs are often characterized as "the runner" for these reasons and more. "He" may block you from communications and also initiate Separation. (Please see the "Super-Simplified Twin Flame Journey – Process Map" for the various stages of the Twin Flame Journey). On the surface, DMs may seem to be "cooler" or more reserved about expressing their love or their feelings.

DFs are typically "warmer" and more relationship-oriented and they are potentially more nurturing on the surface.

They both serve to "trigger" each other in their various interactions throughout the Journey.

The most important thing about the two roles is that they are complementary to one another. One is not "better" than the other. One is not more correct than the other. They both are different sides of the same coin and each one plays a critical role in the Journey to help advance the other in their Soul Growth and Development.

One thing you will need to be careful of is projecting your 3-D programming and prior relationship experiences onto your DM or your DF. This is not that. Old relationship patterns and notions **do not apply** in a real, authentic Twin Flame Journey. In this Journey, you'll need to—and will—re-think everything relating to relationships, fidelity, relationship dynamics, and love.

This is also not a logical Journey. It is a Journey of the heart. Rational, logical, and ego-based thinking will not serve you here. What will serve you is approaching every interaction with unconditional love and surrender to the process ... and surrender to (and trust of) Divine Timing and Divine Intervention.

Super-Simplified Twin Flame Journey – Process Map*

I find it always helps to have a visual. Here is an overly simplified visual of the Journey. Please note: This is a highly simplified visual representation and your own Journey may have even more steps or even be a spiral (repeating steps over and over and not progressing or (seemingly) stopping at a certain point.) This Journey can also continue for months, years. Some people have even been in their Journey for 20 years or more!

Start at the big red arrow.

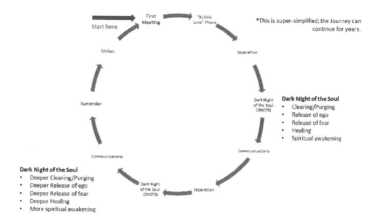

*This is super-simplified; the Journey can continue for years.

First Meeting

"Bubble Love" Phase

Start here

Union

Separation

Surrender

Dark Night of the Soul (DNOTS)

Dark Night of the Soul
- Clearing/Purging
- Release of ego
- Release of fear
- Healing
- Spiritual awakening

Communications

Communications

Dark Night of the Soul
- Deeper Clearing/Purging
- Deeper Release of ego
- Deeper Release of fear
- Deeper Healing
- More spiritual awakening

Dark Night of the Soul (DNOTS)

Separation

The "Bubble Love" Phase

If you ever watched cartoons, and I mean, ANY cartoons and you see the cartoon character who falls in love with another character and you see them floating on air, with little hearts and doves around them, well, that's a pretty realistic visual representation of the "bubble love" phase of the Twin Flame Journey.

After you first meet your Twin, you'll reach a point where you'll feel an incredible bond with this person. They will feel like a missing piece of your heart, or a missing piece of you. You will feel deeply connected. You may be alike in certain ways. You may think alike in certain ways. You may finish each others' sentences. You may make each other laugh or have more fun than you've had in ages, or ever. You'll want to be with this person ALL the time, and it will likely be reciprocated.

You'll care what he or she thinks, above all else. You'll drop everything to be with them, to do things for them, to care for them. You'll recognize that there is very special soul connection between the two of you, a soul bond, that goes way beyond friendship that you most likely haven't felt with anyone else, not even your parents, not your boyfriend or girlfriend, not even your spouse, if you're married. *(For those reading this who are used to regular, 3-D feelings of "puppy love," or infatuation, well, this is similar, but it is not that.)*

This connection is like a tsunami and you're a villager and the strong feelings, the towering wave, are coming right for you. Before you know it, the wave has towered over you, engulfed you, made you its own, washed you up onto shore, and in the meantime, it has turned your village—your entire world—upside down. The landscape will be completely changed. You'll begin to question EVERYTHING.

An easy way to look at it, is take your first love, your first, real love, and times it by, like, 1,000. Maybe more.

This phase of the Journey lasts for weeks for some, months for others, possibly years for others. As for me, mine lasted approximately three months. And then, as quickly as it came, it was gone when Separation set in.

Separation

Following the "Bubble Love" phase, you will have a phase, Separation, that can really happen at any time and at any step along the Journey. It can happen once or many times. It usually starts in the form of "tit-for-tats" going back and forth between the Twins. Or it can stem from major disagreements or when fear is triggered in you or your Twin by something that one or the other does.

The events or happenings that result in Separation can sometimes feel like a "push/pull" dynamic. This is when you "trigger" one another. You'll do or say something that he or she does not like, and vice versa. And you'll call each other on it. It could feel a bit toxic. It may feel like, if you are not truly "coupled together," that you are dating, even when you are not. I often said this of my Twin when I would talk to my best friend about her. I'd say, "You know, it's really weird. It's not like we're dating, but the things we argue or fuss about, it feels like we are." The "relationship" or connection had that intimacy. It had that nature, or that aspect. 100%.

As you're working through these lessons with your Twin, this component of the Journey can trigger or start the phase known as Separation. That is when the two of you separate for a time. It could be days, weeks, months, or even years while you continue working through the issues, each on your own.

The reason for Separation is so that you can work out the issues by yourself, so that you can have the time and space to do that, alone, without any interference. While it is an amazing experience, having a Twin is one of the biggest "distractions" there is. Imagine trying to work through your issues, such as co-dependence (as one example), while you are potentially attached to your Twin in a co-dependent manner. That is just one example. It just wouldn't work. The work has to be done alone, and to completion. This Separation phase can also be used to work through issues related to self-esteem, self-worth, self-acceptance, rejection, abandonment, issues from childhood, trauma, and more. Until these issues are surfaced, acknowledged, purged, and healed, they will be with you and will affect any interaction you will have with anyone else ... your entire life.

One of the purposes of the Twin Flame Journey, as I've mentioned, is to surface and heal these (and other issues). Side note, you may have to work on an issue to heal it for an extended time. You may have to work on a single issue over and over again. But each time, it should get easier and easier. Eventually, with a great deal of self-work, you will be able to heal MOST, if not ALL, of the issues that have plagued you your entire life. In this way, you continue to "purify" yourself by releasing these shadow issues and core wounds. In this way, you are able to become solid and steady in yourself, and not needy of the other person, your Twin. At this point, you will be able to stop chasing. You will be a sovereign being eventually, with the ability to stand on your own two feet. You don't NEED another person, not even your Twin, to complete you. You're complete and whole already.

As I mentioned at the beginning of this book, Separation from my Twin was the worst feeling I have ever felt, the most sad, the most empty, the most devastating.

Separation may feel like the worst hell you've experienced, but after some time (after going through the Dark Night of the Soul—with more details on the following pages), you'll be able to see it less as a hell, and more of a golden opportunity for self-love and soul growth. In short, the Divine is using this time period to "purify" you so that you're ready for Union, both within yourself and with your Twin.

The Dark Night of the Soul (a.k.a. "DNOTS")

The Dark Night of the Soul (also known as "DNOTS," for short) phase typically follows or accompanies the Separation of you and your Beloved, and it can happen one time in your Journey, or several times, or even many times. This will often happen after your Divine Counterpart breaks it off, sends an unmistakably harsh or blunt communication such as "Don't contact me again" and/or "ghosts" you on social media (meaning, they block you on social media or they don't return phone or email messages.)

My Dark Night of the Soul, fortunately, wasn't too bad (generally speaking) in terms of my Journey as compared to others, but I did feel extreme feelings of loss, sadness, missing, and want that I had never felt before to those extents. My emotions are typically on a pretty even keel most of the time, but during my

DNOTS phase, they were very noticeable, like a gut punch that doubles you over...over and over again.

Others on the Journey describe the Dark Night of the Soul as a period of extended confusion, extended bouts of crying, "hell on Earth," "feels like dying," and some even report suicidal thoughts because the relationship with your Beloved has ended (for the time being).

The important thing to note is that while this phase will bring you to your knees, it is a temporary phase and as they say, "This, too, shall pass."

As you go on your Journey, you will become more steady and stable in yourself. This phase helps make you like the mythical creature that burns down to ashes and rises again as mighty Phoenix. It will "burn away" all your self-fear, self-doubt, and insecurities, and it will rebuild you into a newer, better, and even stronger version of yourself.

As one fellow traveler on the Journey said, the DNOTS allowed her to transform her pain into something she didn't think she would survive into a new sense of (and new reality of) self-love and enlightenment. Others describe the final outcome following DNOTS as more beautiful than one can express with words.

Don't lose heart or faith during this devastating stage. It is VERY IMPORTANT to find a friend or confidante who understands and who you can talk to. There are now many Facebook groups where you can meet like-minded people with similar experiences. When you share with them, you'll see patterns and hear commonalities and learn that you're not alone. Few people can understand this Journey. Sometimes only a fellow Twin will understand. Do what you need to in order to cope, but try if you can, to keep it on the healthier side.

Talking with a friend who understands, spending time in nature, meditating, exercising, resting, just letting yourself "be," and being gentle on yourself and treating yourself well are all helpful coping strategies.

No, you're not alone. No, you're not going crazy. You will survive this. I promise. And you'll be stronger and better for having gone through it.

Remember, you signed up for this. Your own soul knew you could handle it and planned this as part of your own Soul-Growth. Yes, you can handle this. Even when it feels like you can't. **You will survive this.**

Am I Going Crazy?

When you first meet your Twin Flame and you have undergone the "Bubble Love" phase, you may still not quite realize "what's hit you" (particularly if you are in another relationship or marriage). When you stop to think about this new connection, this new spark, you may question your sanity and wonder if you're totally losing it. This is because everything you are, everything you've ever known, the way you relate to the world and other people, and the close relationships in your life, will be turned upside down (or turned completely inside and out) from meeting this person.

You'll try to understand, analyze and rationalize this connection. You'll use excuses such as, "This person is fun. I didn't realize what I was missing." Or, "I really admire this person." Or, "Why do I think about this person constantly, day and night, morning and evening?" You'll try to understand with your rational mind. You may even try to minimize it, to shake it off.

But none of that will work. Logic will fall short. And it's because this is a very deep, SOUL connection that cannot be trivialized, minimized, or dismissed. It cannot—and will not—be understood in normal, 3-D, mere mortal sort of way.

The answer to "Am I going crazy?" is that you're not. You're experiencing the Twin Flame connection and starting on the Twin Flame Journey. It's important at this stage that you find a support person or healing modality or healthy coping mechanism to help you make sense of it all. My personal recommendation is, if it's a person you choose to share your experience with (or bounce it off of), pick someone who is more open and spiritual to share with. If you share with just anyone, be prepared to be "shot down," or to hear that perhaps you're infatuated, or you're having a "middle age crisis," and that all of this is in your imagination. There's a big chance it's NOT just your imagination. At this point of your Journey, one of the most important things is to trust your intuition. The same intuition that has never led you wrong. Tap into that. And listen to it. You're gonna need it for this ride.

The Divine Masculine

Adam. Osiris. Jesus. St. Francis of Assisi. Archangel Michael.

One could argue that all of these individuals are the prototypical, archetypical Divine Masculine. He is brave, he is oftentimes a warrior and also exhibits Emperor energies. He has seen many battles and won many battles over countless lifetimes. He has even lost battles. He is courage incarnate. He is a projective force. He is unconditional love in one of its finest forms. He can usually manifest what he wants and needs easily.

In modern (or current) times, he is your Divine Counterpart. But HE may be a "her" in this lifetime. But the current gender does not matter. (More on that later.)

He is your perfect complement, your Divine Mirror.

His strengths are many. He is strong and has well-defined boundaries. He does not typically tolerate a lack of respect from anyone, though he may need to shore up self-respect in himself.

He loves his Divine Feminine (more on her later). He craves her. They are divinely tied to one another by forces beyond our full understanding, connected by the mysterious red thread. (More on that later.)

He may not be fully aware of the Twin Flame Journey YET. He is typically the runner in the Journey, but not always.

At his best, he is brave, strong, and fierce. He is powerful beyond measure in every way, but he may not realize it yet. Through this Journey, he will come to realize his own inner strength and power.

At his worst, to simplify, he can be somewhat controlling, aggressive, and/or manipulative. A veneer of bravado can mask tender insecurities. See below for the comparison between the healed Divine Masculine and the wounded Divine Masculine.

Healed Divine Masculine	Wounded Divine Masculine
Brave	Aggressive
Strong	Controlling
Vulnerable	Hard Exterior or Indifferent
Protector	Controlling

"Safe Harbor"	Manipulative
Loving	Aloof/Guarded
Relaxed; Open; Acting Out of Unconditional Love, Not Out of Ego	Running

The Divine Feminine

Eve. Isis. Mary Magdalene. Claire of Assisi.

One could argue that all of these individuals are the prototypical, archetypical Divine Feminine. She is maternal, she is loving. She exhibits Empress energies. She is often a caregiver or nurturer. She exhibits untold inner strength. She is love incarnate, also unconditional love in one of its finest forms. She is a receptive force.

In modern (or current) times, she is your Divine Counterpart. But SHE may be a "him" in this lifetime. But the current gender does not matter. (More on that later.)

She is your perfect complement, your Divine Mirror.

Her strengths are many. She is strong and is very protective of those she loves. She protects her loved ones, her nest.

She loves her Divine Masculine (you can read more on that in the earlier pages). She craves him. They are divinely tied to one another by forces beyond our full understanding, connected by the mysterious red thread. (More on that later.)

She is usually the first to become aware of the Twin Flame connection and the Journey, but not always. She is typically the "chaser," but not always.

At her best, she is nurturing, maternal, the source of all creation. Like the Divine Masculine, she, too, is powerful beyond measure in every way, but it's likely she will not realize it until she is well into her Journey. Through the lessons in the Journey, she will come to fully realize her own inner strength and power. She will not tolerate B.S. or suffer fools easily.

At her worst, to simplify, she can be co-dependent and/ or needy, manipulative, or controlling. See below for the comparison between the healed Divine Feminine and the wounded Divine Feminine.

Healed Divine Feminine	Wounded Divine Feminine
Nurturer	Controlling
Maternal	Overprotective
Vulnerable	Hard or Indifferent Exterior
Loving	Smothering
Strong	Manipulative or Demanding

Relaxed; In Surrender; Confident; Acting Out of Unconditional Love	Chasing
Calm; Steady	Dramatic or Overly Dramatic

Why We Chase and Why We Run

Why We Chase, As Divine Feminines

Why do we chase? It's an important question to ask yourself if you're a Divine Feminine, and I've only been able to answer it after several years of being on this Journey.

I believe we, as Divine Feminines, chase our Twin, our Divine Counterpart, because we are so acclimated to the typical 3-D approach to love and relationships. To obtain love, we believe we must court it, we must follow our emotions to their natural equivalent of actions to cement the connection, to try to "make it real." We then try to "wrestle it to the ground." But on the Twin Flame Journey, things don't work as they do in the 3-D, and your usual methods that work so well to attract someone to you and to keep them there, don't work at all, much to your dismay.

Many of us are so desperate for true love and affection, that when we think we sense it, we run toward it with all our energy and all our might. We will do practically anything to try to make it real (at least, as real as it is in our own hearts and minds.)

I also believe we chase because we are not confident in our own skins. We do not love ourselves in a sufficient way, and so we are always seeking love from somewhere outside of us, just like we are always seeking validation outside of us. We don't yet know that true love and true acceptance starts with ourselves, and we must love ourselves wholly and completely first before anyone else can—or will. We must feel whole inside of ourselves before we can join with another.

Another fact about chasing is that we do it as a form of (attempted) control. It's just the truth of the matter. I think perhaps I didn't want to admit this to myself for a long time, but it finally came to me recently that it is another way for us to try to control our Divine Partner, to try to control the Journey, to make ourselves feel more comfortable, to exert some power over a situation that makes us feel powerless. Once we recognize this fact and admit it, then we can start the process of true surrender and release, and "get out of our own ways" so that everything can unfold naturally, in Divine Timing.

I also sense that we chase on the Journey (time and again) to keep it feeling "real." We want our Twin Flame to acknowledge the connection, to admit they feel the same way that we do. We feel we must accomplish this above all else (again, as proof of the connection). When this doesn't happen, it can trigger us and send us into spirals of self-doubt, sadness, and even depression. For more on this topic, please reference the section of this book entitled, "You Do You."

Why We Run, as Divine Masculines

I am not a Divine Masculine, but I will do my best to address why Divine Masculines run, as I understand it, from everything I have personally experienced and everything I have read and heard on the Journey. Many, including those who self-identify as Divine Masculines, say they run because the Twin Flame connection is too intense. It brings up too much in their emotional field: too much doubt, too many questions. Also, they feel they're not ready for such a "big love." They're not ready to experience such intense emotions and the deep spiritual connection. In fact, some of them may not be ready for any type of real love, or authentic love. He or she may have gotten used to the 3-D templates of love and sex and that is all they have learned to expect or want. A new experience, or the potential of a new experience, perhaps "blows their minds" and they don't know what to do with it.

They may also run because of certain 3-D realities, such as when the other Twin has a partner, a spouse, kids, a family. It may be too messy or inconvenient to disrupt (or seemingly disrupt) a family unit that is on the outside, by all accounts, a "happy family." It takes real strength to feel these intense emotions and not to act on them, so we really should give Divine Masculines a lot of credit with regard to self-control. They are masters of self-control.

There can also be family issues on the part of the Divine Masculine that he or she must face, like perhaps the concern that relationship won't be accepted by their own family because of things like the gender, race, or socioeconomic status of their Twin, or the age difference between him or her and the Twin.

Another key factor of why Divine Masculines run is because they may associate the karma and karmic lessons that come as a result of the Journey, with the Divine Feminine. It may appear to them that she caused it all, or that she is at fault, or that she did something to bring all of this upon the both of them when, in fact, it is a collaborative Journey and a collaborative, co-creative "project" between the two Twins for the benefit of both of them. This co-creation is designed so that both souls can experience these karmic lessons and process through them so that they can both resolve issues and achieve true Soul Growth.

In fact, some Twins may experience all of the above. These obstacles, while huge, are not insurmountable, as many Twins in Union can attest. Sometimes it requires a miracle, or many miracles, but if you're like me, you believe in miracles. You've seen them firsthand. This Journey is no different.

A Word About Gender Roles

Society has conditioned us to place great priority on gender roles. Just think about it. In school. In church. At work. In the home. Your gender role typically largely predicates how you will be treated by others, and how you should act.

The truth is, in God's World, in the 5-D, gender roles are not important. I understand that this statement may "trigger" some of you, but that is societal and religious programming that you must examine for yourself and meditate upon (if this statement triggers you).

In God's World, and in the world of the Twin Flame Journey, God, Archangel Michael, and all the angels (or spirit guides or whomever you look to for comfort in times of trouble), do not particularly care about gender identity or expression. That is a 3-D construct.

What this means is that truly, if you are male, your Twin Flame could be female, or she could be male, or she could even be another gender expression. (There are many different types of gender expressions today, but we will not go into them here).

If you are female, your Twin could be male, or she could be female, or even another gender expression.

This was (and is) a big shocker and surprise for those Twins on the Journey who had previously identified as heterosexual or straight. I know countless people who have learned that their Twin upon meeting him or her, much to their surprise, is the same sex as them! For many, this is a difficult adjustment and they have had to "shed" much of their societal programming to figure out how to best deal with this Twin Flame relationship or Journey.

God and the guides, if you listen, are very clear on this subject. They don't place the same value on certain things as we do (gender expression, money, etc.) The values are radically different.

On your Journey, if you have "negative" feelings or emotions associated with being "twinned" with a person who is of the same sex is you, that will be another trigger or emotional hurdle that you will both need to overcome as part of your journey to wholeness.

This hurdle may be too big to overcome for some, and they may decide, through "free will" to not pursue the Journey any longer...it may be just too much for them.

But many are able to overcome the societal and religious programming to have happy and healthy relationships with their Twin. (By the way, the "relationship" doesn't always have to be physical. It can be, but it doesn't have to be.)

As I told three Episcopal priests one night as they were trying to "convert" me from being gay to straight (a "surprise" meeting that went for hours that I did not know was going to happen), I calmly explained to them…"Would you agree that Jesus is the 'star' or the centerpiece of the Bible you use in this church?" And they said, "Yes." I said, "Show me in the Bible where Jesus says one bad or "negative" thing about homosexuals." They were speechless. They had no answer for that one.

The truth is, a statement from Jesus such as this doesn't exist. Any statements against being gay were written in the Bible by men. Men who didn't want the patriarchy or the current system to be "upset" or disrupted by forces that were different from the norm. The church wrote it in for a variety of reasons that we won't go into here. And it's remained that way (mostly) until today.

One of the very important things this Journey is trying to teach is the loosening (or total elimination) of restrictions. You are entitled by our Creator to freedom. You are not intended to be shackled by anyone or anything. Not by a boyfriend. Not by a girlfriend. Not by a spouse. Not by a job. Not by social media. Not by your neighbors' or family's expectations. Not by a role you are playing for some person. All these parameters, these limitations, are also 3-D constructs. We are meant to be bigger than we are (in every way). Within reason, you are entitled to FREEDOM and you are entitled to EXPANSION. You are a wholly sovereign being entitled to live your life the way you want (within reason). Like the butterfly that flits from flower to flower, the blue jay that swoops through the sky, the hawk soaring above, above all, **you are meant to be free.**

You may ruminate on what this means to you, but once you realize you are shackled and those shackles have only been placed upon you by YOU, then you realize that you are the one with the power to release them.

Yes, that Divine Power is in YOU. You are the painter of your own masterpiece, the sailor of your ship, the captain of your everything. Don't let anyone minimize you, restrain you, "put you in a corner," or diminish you in any way. That's not how it's supposed to be.

A Word About Protecting
Your Energy

I have a very good friend that works at a large national coffee chain as a barista. She is both an empath and a light worker, and dealing with the various people that come in (imagine the numbers of people), she says it's easy to pick up on their energy, and then you end up carrying it with you.

One of the things that is most important as an empath or a light worker, is that you consciously decide when to open and close your chakras so you are not picking up and carrying other people's energy with you as you go about your day.

This is important because as you continue and progress on your Journey, you will begin to see and realize how you are connected energetically not only to your Twin, but to others, as well. If you are an Empath and a lightworker, at times, this can get overwhelming, so you need to know how to properly manage and protect your own energy.

Your statement can be as simple as: "I choose to open my chakras to be more in alignment with [NAME] or feeling, like [LOVE] at this moment." Say you are working on a healing process for yourself or another, you can consciously open them up so that you can get a better result with you or your person you are working with (or on).

Then, when you are done, and this is most important whether you're a Reiki healer or you are just talking with a friend or friends, you can say, "I choose to close my chakras so I can go about my day (and/or operate fully and functionally in the world).

Otherwise, your energy is wide open, for anyone to access, tap into or "glom onto." If you don't actively and consciously work to protect yourself and manage this energy, it can build up over time and get overwhelming.

I did not even know this was possible until my Reiki Master informed me of it. (Thank you. You know who you are!)

Wouldn't this be a useful tool for every human to know? Like, kids in elementary school should be taught this. How many people do unthinkable things because they are carrying others' energy (or feeling others' energy) that is not their own? School and life would be structured very differently if we all knew and practiced just a little bit of proper "energy management."

Synchronicities, Significant Numbers and Mirror Numbers

Synchronicities, significant numbers, and mirror numbers are a huge part of the Twin Flame Journey and process. What are synchronicities, you may ask? Well, if you don't know already, synchronicities are seeing numbers, dates, initials, or repeating numbers or hearing or seeing songs, song lyrics or phrases that remind you of your Twin Flame. (Some examples would be, seeing 11:11 on the clock, 2:22, 3:33, etc.) Or seeing your Twin's year of birth or dates of birth. Synchronicities are a critical part of the process. Your guides will use these synchronicities in several ways:

1) To provide a signal or a message that you're awake and on the right track, whatever your path may be.

2) To help you feel greater closeness to, and connection to, your Twin Flame.

3) To show you the power of miracles and that anything is possible.

4) To help you re-imagine the world in new and different ways and see possibility.

5) To keep you focused on your Journey when you become distracted.

6) To pull you back in, to re-engage you, if you are getting tired of the process or doubting the process.

7) To bring you back in if you decide to quit the Journey.

One of my best friends, who also happens to be on the Twin Flame Journey, likens synchronicities to "bread crumbs" that we follow to guide us on our Journey, to keep us in constant contact and connection to it.

In a recent guided meditation that I took into the quantum, or higher realms, I received a message from Spirit that referred to these "bread crumbs." And the message was clear, when you encounter these signs: "Don't doubt the bread crumbs."

My friend (who is also a Twin) also draws parallels between the Twin Flame Journey and a marathon. If you've ever run a half-marathon or marathon, it can be daunting to think about those 13 miles or 26.2 miles. So, the marathon organizers will put rewards between you and the finish line to keep you going. At certain points, there's a water tent or a beer tent.

When you're running, you'll often feel like quitting, but you'll say to yourself, "If I can just get to the water tent." It keeps you going. And before you know it, you've pushed yourself to run another mile. Before you know it, you have a whole lot of miles behind you. Even when you thought you couldn't do it, and you felt you couldn't carry on. Yep, synchronicities are a lot like that and you'll begin to see lots of them as you continue on your path. Sometimes you'll see a lot, sometimes you'll see a little, but they're always there, if you just open up to it and pay attention.

Here are some common numbers that you'll see that are considered "synchronicities." Have you seen any of these lately (or even today)?

Synchronicity	Basic Meanings
11:11, 1:11, 1111, 111, 11	• 11:11 is "The Twin Flame Number" • A master number • The bigger picture • The Divine Path • "Code of activation" • Take a breath, quiet your mind, and listen to the messages that source energy has for you now • Evidence of alignment with God, Universe, spirit • Connection between humans and God, Universe, spirit • An auspicious sign • Oneness; unity • Angels or spirit guides are close by • You are a divine aspect of the Creator • A reminder that you came here for a purpose and to leave the Earth better than you found it when you were born • Tremendous opportunities
2:22, 2222, 222, 22	• A new path is opening up for you • Be aware and open to blessings • A wake-up call of divine intervention • You are guided, supported, and loved • Raise your vibration • Confirms your ability to manifest rapidly • Pay attention to your thoughts • Stay positive

	• Couple your unique gifts with that of your Twin to also help raise the vibration of humanity and Earth • Number of Union; number of the twins • You're on the right track and in the right place at the right time • Listen to your intuition • Trust and stay focused on what you want, rather than what you DON'T WANT • Everything is working out according to Divine Will for the highest and greatest good
3:33, 3333, 333, 33	• Reminder that the Divine, Angels, spirit guides and ascended masters are working with you on a number of levels • Get clear about what you want • Ask for help • Work with Spirit to co-create what you want
4:44, 4444, 444, 44	• Your angels are with you and supporting you • They are assisting you with unconditional love • All is well • The number of stability and marriage; Union • Listen to your intuition • Ask for help

5:55, 5555, 555, 55	<ul><li>Indicates arrival of good things for Twin Flames</li><li>"Angel number"</li><li>Manifestation of joy and happiness</li><li>Indicates time to "reap the rewards" of the good work you have put forth</li><li>You are in synch with your true self</li><li>Things in life are starting to shift to be more in alignment with "the real you"</li><li>Your new path will be revealed one step at a time</li><li>Your life has ultimate significance</li><li>Wholeness of creation in human form</li><li>A major change is coming your way</li><li>Major changes are not bad; they are good; they are opportunity</li><li>Be open; stay positive</li><li>Choose what is in alignment with your best and highest self and best and highest purpose</li><li>Co-create positive change</li></ul>
6666, 666, 66	<ul><li>This number has been portrayed historically in a Biblical sense as the number of all things evil, but in our Journey, it means something very different</li><li>Wake up to your higher self</li><li>Guidance to listen to your heart, not your head</li><li>Number of unconditional love</li></ul>

	• Indicator that you could be too focused on matters associated with the 3-D • Call to return to balance • Call to be more present • Release fear and uncertainty and turn worries over to God, Universe, spirit • Elevate your thoughts • Return to balance • Return your focus to love and unconditional love
7777, 777, 77	• You're on the right track • You've been hearing and listening to divine guidance • You've been taking steps to heal and improve your life, and it's working
8888, 888, 88	• The number of wealth and abundance • The number of infinity • Embrace changes and continue working on your life purpose • You're becoming more aligned with prosperity and your divine purpose • When you embrace the changes, they can positively impact your life
9999, 999, 99	• The number of completion, or being close to completion • Embrace the changes so that you can get to work on your life purpose • You are a lightworker • It's time to live in alignment with the Divine and with your Soul Purpose

0000, 000, 00	• Your energy in every moment has an impact on what you're creating • Stay positive and think about what you want to co-create • This is the number of infinite possibilities • Open your heart • Improve and increase your vibration • Connect with the Divine

Mirror Numbers

Mirror numbers are exactly what you might imagine, numbers that are the exact same when you are reading them from left to right, or right to left. Some examples would be:

- 11:11
- 12:21
- 12:26
- 10:01
- 1:01, 2:02, 3:03, etc.

Mirror numbers can represent a connection to the spirit world, to your guides. Many believe it is a way that the spirit guides capture your attention. Just like synchronicities, pay attention to what you were thinking about whenever you see these numbers. Through intuition, you may be able to discern what meaning the mirror numbers have for you.

Mirroring

One of the very important components of the Twin Flame Journey is mirroring. You may not realize it at first, but being Divine Counterparts, you do share the same soul and part, if not all, of the emotional body and energy field. Therefore, what one Twin feels, the other may feel. This seems to happen more and more at certain times, when "the veil" is very thin.

A friend of mine and I learned this as we compared notes along our Journey, and also on countless posts on Twin Flame Facebook group pages where one person would say, "I felt so lost and confused last night, but it came out of nowhere, and I knew 'it wasn't me.'" Meaning: The other twin's feelings would unexpectedly come rushing into that person's energy/emotion/physical field and you would feel those emotions.

I, too, experienced this with my Twin. One night, when I had been feeling very confident about the Journey, suddenly, a feeling of confusion washed over me, and try though I might to find the source of this feeling/emotion, I could not explain it. I had the urge to journal about it to process it, but it came and went pretty quickly, so by the time I was getting ready to express my emotions and attempting to process it through writing it all out, it had passed as quickly as it came on. The next morning, I awoke to the thought of: "Oh, I am not confused at all. I am clear as a bell on this Journey and what it means and where I am in the process." That is just one example of mirroring.

For yet another friend of mine, she is the most relaxed person you will ever meet, but, she frequently feels her Twin. Feelings of anxiety wash over her pretty frequently. She says she knows, without a doubt, they aren't her emotions, but rather, those of her Twin. Yet another of my friends has gotten physically (stomach) ill out of nowhere and it passed as quickly as it came. She later found out her Twin had had the same thing happen that same night, even though they weren't together and hadn't been together physically. They hadn't seen one another in a while. They were mirroring even a physical symptom!

One of the ways I've attempted to work through this is … once I consciously knew … I mean really knew … that my Twin and I shared the same emotional body and energy field, I started not only drawing Oracle/

Tarot cards for myself to guide me on my Journey, but I would, pull cards for her, immediately after. In this way, I was able to tap into her energy and experience at this point in time, even in physical and communication separation. This was extremely helpful over time.

Additionally, I watched as the cards began to "mirror" each other...meaning if I pulled "Trust Your Intuition" for me one day, I would pull that same card for my Twin the next day. When the Journey first began, I knew intuitively that my Twin was always like four to six months behind me on the Journey and in her soul progression/soul development/karmic release, etc. That time difference started to close up a bit gradually and it was like, "I know she's three months behind." Now, we are more closely in alignment in that I am pulling the same cards for her as I have for myself, in the same day or a day apart from one another. Sometimes this also happens on the exact same day when we receive the same card! This happens very frequently. Out of 44 cards, that, to me, is beyond a coincidence.

Mirroring even extends to our dream states. When you are sleeping and you have had a dream, you'll often wonder if your Twin felt or experienced that same dream. The truth is, they often do. They may experience it in a slightly different way, but often, you'll have the same (or similar) dreams. Dreaming about your Twin serves to strengthen the soul connection, the magnetic pull between the two of you, and helps to enhance the lure from one Twin to another. I know this because upon waking after having a dream about my Twin, I feel more bonded to her than ever. I have also been able to confirm she and I are having the same or a similar dream using other methods of divination.

The process of mirroring can even extend into the 3-D. What one Twin is experiencing in real life (as some examples, a headache, being sick to your stomach or an ailment on a particular part of your body, such as a rash). Believe it or not, but these physical ailments can mirror over to your Twin as well. The ailment may not be exactly the same in terms of severity, but it does happen occasionally. (You may think this falls into the "Believe It Or Not" category, but my Twin friends and I have experienced real world, actual 3-D "proof" of this phenomena).

These are all examples of how the "mirroring" works, in my experience. This is useful to remember because it helps you become more closely aligned and in tune with your Twin. This is particularly helpful if you are feeling any anger or resentment toward him or her. He or she is truly an extension of you. Being mad at your partner is like being mad at yourself! The concept of mirroring also expands your scope of understanding beyond yourself. In times of Separation, this can be particularly useful and can also help to reduce frustration and misunderstandings, which only prolong the Journey and may work to prolong your coming into Union in the 3-D. (This is not always the ultimate goal of the Journey, by the way, but we'll delve more into that later.)

Telepathy

Connecting in the fifth dimension is a way you can tap into your Twin Flame's thoughts and dreams.

You may ask yourself whether telepathy with your Twin is really possible or if it is really happening. Have no doubt. It is. This has been confirmed by many Twins. When you become frustrated because of no communication in the 3-D, it's important to remember, you can talk to your Twin anytime, telepathically. How do you do this, you ask? It's simple. It's as simple as talking to your friend or your mother or a family member.

1) Think of your Beloved anytime. Or you can do this before bedtime, as well, to "meet up" in the dreamspace.

2) Set the intention that you want to communicate telepathically with your Twin or that you want to have dreams of him or her. You can say something

as simple as, "I intend to..." or "I set my intention to communicate in the 5-D with [NAME]." Or, "I intend to dream about my Twin." Or even a request, if you are so inclined, a prayer. You can pray and ask for connection with your Twin in thoughts or dreams.

3) Then, in the immortal words of John Mayer, "Say what you need to say." I've communicated short phrases up to the contents of entire letters to my Twin during the daytime and in the evenings, too.

This communication is bi-directional and can help you continue to remain close to your Twin. It can allow you to convey important things you need to say, even when you are in Separation. The best part? You can do this anytime. You'll soon start to see (or hear) proof from your Twin that this is working, or you may start to see progress in your Twin Flame Journey.

Astral Sex/Astral Lovemaking

Just like communicating with your Twin in the 5-D, you can also be intimate with him or her in the astral plane. This can happen on its own, or you can initiate it, too. It works exactly the same as telepathy (please reference the Telepathy section). It's easy and it works to attract your Twin even more to you in the 3-D. The steps are the same as telepathy:

1) Think of your Beloved.

2) Set the intention that you want to be intimate with your Twin or express your love in a physical way. You can say something as simple as, "I intend" or "I set my intention to be with (or connect to) my Twin intimately in the 5-D."

3) Then you can imagine yourself kissing or touching him or her. You can let it unfold naturally, just like using your imagination.

4) If you want to throw some extra "spice" into the equation, you can also touch yourself or imagine yourself touching him or her.

5) Just go with the flow.

I wasn't sure this could ever feel as good as being with a human being in the 3-D, but believe me, it is. This ability to be intimate and make love with your Twin in the 5-D is a valuable (and enjoyable) tool to have in your toolbox.

If you're in doubt, maybe just try it and see.

If you're not comfortable with it, that's okay, too. Maybe it's not for everyone. And people have varying levels of comfort with sex and personal intimacy.

The 3-D programming against all types of sex and sexual expression, particularly in terms of religion, can be very strong. This is ESPECIALLY true if your Twin is of the same gender as you. If this is the case for you, it's important to re-examine your thoughts on sex and intimacy. It could be that you have blocks in place that are preventing you from being as free as you can be (and need to be and want to be) with regard to sexual pleasure and enjoyment. It is my personal belief that God/Source gave us sex as a gift, not only to pro-create, but to show (and to share) our love. When you have a healthy attitude about sex, and a healthy respect for it, it can truly be an enjoyable part of your Journey until you reach Union with your Twin Flame (and definitely, AFTER you reach Union with your Twin).

The "Gas Station Example": Getting Out of the Way

Speaking of prolonging the Journey, there are things to NOT DO while you are on your Journey. This came to me through a brilliant "real-world" example that I experienced as I was writing this book. I had a strange incident at a convenience store when I was trying to put gas in my car.

I could not get my card to process on the pump I was on, so I went in to the attendant and (as I was in a rush) looking out the window, I saw a large number 1 on the pump where my car appeared to be. I asked for $25 on Pump Number One. Little did I know, because of odd signage, I was actually at Pump Number Two when I asked.

So when I came back out, I happened to notice that the other pump (the "real Pump Number One") had the $25 on it, not my pump. Then a guy pulled up into that space to get gas, and I was like, "Hey, can you help me out?" Of course, he was ignoring me thinking I was asking for money (as does frequently happen at the gas station ... so I understood his hesitation to answer me). I finally got him to pay attention to me and asked if I could pull in to the slot that had the $25 showing on the monitor. He understood what had happened and then agreed to move...and I pulled in.

Little did I know, at the exact same time or right before that, the clerk (with a very long line of customers) noticed my mistake and was switching the $25 back to the other original pump where I had been parked. Of course, when I tried to pump the gas where I was, the meter was sitting on $0 and wouldn't do anything. So I went back in to the lady and though I was feeling somewhat exasperated, I told her it wasn't working. And she said, "I saw your mistake and so I changed pumps for you, but then you had already moved to the other gas spot as I was doing that."

I then asked her to please cancel out all transactions so that we could start all over again. Luckily, she wasn't hating on me too bad and exhibited "Employee of the Month" behaviors in our interaction. I asked her to please put me on an entirely NEW pump, Pump Number 3. So we processed the transaction all over again.

When I walked out to Pump 3, the meter was sitting on $75, so I thought she had mistakenly run my transaction three times. So I walked back in, and I, starting to unravel at the seams a bit, was like, "What the heck... it's on $75. And I cannot put $75 worth of gas in my car, even if I wanted to." By this time, we're both getting a bit frustrated. Her Employee of the Month demeanor was starting to wither away, but she was able to retain her pleasant demeanor. She says," Oh! That $75 was for the previous transaction before you. Try again."

So I did, and it FINALLY worked. I later wondered why it took me FOREVER to get gas at that time and I wondered if the Universe was trying to show me patience once again (this seems to be an underlying ... er, overarching theme of my Journey). But as I continued to think on it, because it wasn't at all a subtle lesson, it occurred to me that the Universe or Source Energy is trying to show me an example of how I "show up" to life and to the Journey most of the time.

Like, if something doesn't work or doesn't progress as quickly as I would like, I swoop in to try to fix it. And when I do that, I don't allow others (or Spirit/Universe/ Source) to help me remedy the situation.

Correlating to the Twin Flame Journey for me and for us all, perhaps when you don't get the results you want, rather than allowing the Universe/Source Energy to do its thing, you jump right into the mechanics of everything, jamming it all up. The lady was trying to fix my mistake unbeknownst to me. But then I took over and tried to fix it all myself, thinking *I* was the more efficient and competent answer. And in the "gas station example," it just got worse and more time-delayed from there.

If I had to guess, I would say, my guides are saying (in this example and also in a more overarching and probably emphatic way):

"Get the hell out of the way. You think you know what's best, but you really don't. You think you know how to fix it, but you really don't. Stop trying to micromanage everything and to control everything. Because you are not allowing us to play our role in this. Your involvement is actually mucking the whole thing up."

True story. And a valuable lesson.

"You Do You"

"You do you." These were about the three most heart-breaking words I ever heard, and I heard them from my beloved Divine Counterpart. My Twin Flame. My Divine Masculine.

They came after a particularly harrowing series of backs- and-forths. After a long series of triggering, clearing, processing, and going back and forth.

At the time, they felt like the worst words I could ever hear, coming from her. Naturally, I was broken-hearted and spent what felt like weeks thereafter feeling sorry for myself, feeling dejected, rejected, abandoned, kicked-to-the-curb and subsequently, licking my wounds. I don't quite think I've ever been wounded quite so badly by three simple and direct words.

My TWIN FLAME has always been totally, 100% blunt with me. Generally speaking, I was used to it. I appreciated the refreshing honesty over the last two years of our unconventional friendship/relationship (with so much going on underneath the surface). But this time, it just stung ("stung" is actually an understatement).

After all, prior to that, I had, to the extent I could, poured out a written appeal to her, saying (along the lines of), "...please acknowledge this connection. You know it and I know it. You participated in it, and all of this, just as much as I did." [Leaving out about a hundred complex layers to the situation, which we all know and struggle with, things like a small town, a karmic partner, a successful business with a karmic partner, not to mention – and especially the crown jewels of it all -- two young children, a host of people who just couldn't understand (including parents on all sides), pent-up, unacknowledged homophobia, hometown mentality, social connections that just do not and would not understand or support a new and unconventional relationship, whispers behind our backs, etc. etc. etc. You all know the drill and it ain't pretty.]

And despite my heartfelt appeal (which I suppose was intended to awaken her), I was met with (despite about a thousand overt, 3-D actions over two years that screamed to the contrary), "[NAME], I've never been attracted to you, I'm not attracted to you. I can't do this back-and-forth anymore. *Please...*" [I must admit the "Please" just kind of made me stop in my tracks and pause. I felt so much compassion for her reading that portion of the note, knowing I was overloading her without even meaning to. It was all so well-intentioned, but it just seemed to all fall apart with this latest email exchange.]

And, then the mic-drop. She wrote to me: *"You do you."*

Just wow.

So now, looking at this statement and really absorbing it ... now, months later, it FINALLY feels different. Refreshing. Liberating even. Because I took those three months since the time of Separation and lack of communication to really take her advice (it didn't feel like advice at the time, honestly; it felt like a blistering admonition).

I used that time and space during Separation to double-down and to take a cold, hard look at me, warts and all. The last months have been filled with meditations, guided meditations, purging, crying, clearing, singing, screaming, punching my bed with my fists so hard (both actually and in my mind over and over again), writing, journaling, Oracle card pulling, tarot card reader visiting, reading about a million posts on Quora, watching reads from TF Enchantress (now Sylvia Escalante), and so many more that I truly believe I could write a thesis on the subject by now (almost). (I suppose this book is now my thesis.) And it's an evolving story. At least I believe it is all still unfolding.

What did I learn by "me doing me?" That I am beautiful, honorable, spiritual, honest, following my bliss, that I

HAVE been trusting my intuition, my emotions, and my heart and following them all along (and I know they will never, ever lead me wrong). That I am not sorry, nor do I apologize for having been tapped on the shoulder for this Journey. (Or signing up for it, whenever I did.) Begs the question: *Did someone else sign me up for this, after all?*

So, these handful of years have been the wildest, most cosmic, most interesting, happiest, most in love, most thrilling, most depressing, most agonizing, most blissful 48 months or so of my life (aside from conceiving, birthing, and raising two beautiful children). My Soul Growth and personal expansion is really mind-blowing. The soul progression is very quick and earth-shaking at times. My karmic partner of 20 years has said, "I just can't keep up with you."

My karmic partner also said to me recently, when I said, "I just NEED to know that I am fulfilling my soul purpose and mission." She replied: "Now why would you want to go and do something like that?" And then, despite struggling with that relationship and balancing the new coming in through the Twin Flame partnership, you just know. *You just really know.* Sticking with a current situation will no longer work.

Look, if my Twin Flame never comes around in this lifetime or another, I am still for certain that we are co-collaborating together in ways that are beautiful (though they don't always seem or feel that way!) I love her unconditionally. I told her so maybe like two or three weeks after we met. The statement came out without forethought, but it was true, and I meant it, and I had absolutely no idea why I was texting those words to her (at that point in time). But now I do, I really do.

I have finally surrendered to the fact, that while that it will suck, it will also be OKAY. I am learning to trust in the process more, trust the Universe more. I have to believe the Universe is benevolent and would never do anything to truly harm me (or us), and is only doing that which can bring us to a lighter and brighter place. Kind of like the Extreme Sports version of Soul Growth.

With this new perspective, "You do you" actually feels good. It feels light and bright. I do truly feel I have gained a great deal more soul love. I am doing what I want to do. I am happy with my new pursuits, like stepping out of the shadows, being vulnerable, and writing this book, and thinking about and planning a non-profit I want to start in my local community. That is pretty much filling me up right now, along with being the best parent and person I can be. I have hope – and know – deeply that everything is going to be alright now that I am "doing me" just fine.

I think she would be proud. I think she would like the new me. Time will tell. Bottom line: I did me. And I am still in love with her. Maybe more than ever.

A Letter to my Divine Masculine:
A True Love Story

(Note: This is a letter I wrote, never sent. But I would like to.)

Dear Divine Masculine:

I haven't been in communications with you, either in 3-D or 5-D for months. I wonder what you're feeling and experiencing right now. Though you're still in my thoughts, pretty much 24/7 as you've been for each and every day of three-and-a-half years now...

The night before last (February 10, 2019), I fought and thrashed energetically all throughout the night. I wondered upon waking, what on earth was going on throughout the night. Something definitely was, but no clear messages came from it, so I am still in the dark.

Since I don't "feel" you quite as much, I am trying to purposefully keep my vibration high and so I thought what better way to do that than to write you a love note.

I met you in March 2017 and saw you a handful of times before you were the one who actually awakened me the evening of the 22nd (note the repetitive 2s … one meaning is "walking the path to unity") on a beautiful summer month, my birthday month. At the time, we were in the signs of both of our births (Cancer). You came up to me at my car following an event at my business. You came in close, close enough to feel your breath. I practically fled out of there, knowing my karmic partner (of 18 years), who had just left, would be home waiting and wondering. I felt so confused by the flood of emotions, the feeling that you had just awakened something in me that I didn't even know was there.

Looking back, I wish I had stayed.

One night, you were hanging out at my house with my karmic and my best friend. I had gone out of town to see some friends. When you FaceTimed me (or ended up on FaceTime – I don't recall exactly how it happened), my heart soared. I was grinning ear to ear. About YOU. I could have stayed on that call with you all night. My relationship with my karmic faded into the background and YOU were the only one I wanted to talk to that night.

Then, fast-forward, about a million texts and a million emoticons that still make me smile thinking of them.

Fast-forward also to triggering and release at key intervals of our unconventional "relationship." And then an apology from you from time to time for taking things out on me that you knew I didn't deserve. Even those apologies made me smile. I know you so deeply and thoroughly, and I don't know how I know, but I always knew just when you were going to show up unannounced, and I always knew when you were going to apologize. I knew/sensed everything before it even happened (and I had never had claircognizance, that level of intuition and advance knowing, before).

I still look for your car, for you, every time I pass by the turn to your house. (Thinking of the song by Babyface, "I Only Think of You on Two Occasions" ... that's "day and night" that says it all so well).

I wish you would communicate in the 3-D, but I've stopped looking for an email in my inbox (or a text on my phone), knowing that you are doing the work you are supposed to be doing right now, away from me and in Separation. And I am also acknowledging that this wonderful connection we shared could be over, but I am remaining focused on the old phrase, "Don't be sorry that it's over. Be grateful that it happened."

My relationship with you has been the greatest one of my life. The one that rivaled every epic tale or movie (storylines that I previously thought were "cheesy" and could never happen in real life). For this is the relationship that has pushed me to utmost Soul Growth, self-reflection, self-development, and self-love.

I love you as truly, madly, and deeply as anyone ever could. I am your sun, and you are my moon. I wore everything on my sleeve in the bright of day; you preferred the nighttime, the shadows, the guarded secrecy. I used to hate it, but now I accept that part of you. The yin to my yang.

I now know that the sun and moon are interdependent and cannot exist without the other. I try to shine as brightly as I can for you. I've received the message from Spirit, from my guides, that we Divine Counterparts are like the sun and therefore, must let our lights shine as brightly as we can, like a lighthouse for our Divine Partner, in the hopes he/she will make his way home to us at long last.

If you walk through my door again, I know that I will crumble into your arms, for I am tired and needing you, needing your strength, your spirit, your confidence, your resolve, your warrior spirit. I know I can be great— and healthy—for you. I know I can give you the balance you need and seek. I will do what I do best, nurture you, care for you, and protect you in my own way, as you protect me.

But all those feelings are not off in the ether somewhere; they are right here, right now. I am loving you, caring for you, and protecting you and I hope you can feel it from me. It is among the highest of purposes for me, the infinite blessing, and I am basking in all this Journey has brought me. I hope you feel the same way, too. But until then, I will send you all my love, all my light, everything I have, for we are bound together in a beautiful connection that defies all words and even time and space.

Managing Through Life Dynamics Along the Journey

Homewrecker. That's the term my karmic partner had taken to calling my Divine Counterpart, my beloved Twin Flame, as the Journey was unfolding around us.

It cut deeply every time she said it, because I knew it just didn't feel right. It wasn't right. It felt simple and small, and took something very beautiful and made it, to use a 1990s term, "tawdry," ... salacious, even.

One night it came to me in my dreamspace, that point of time and space between waking and a dream. It was a conversation I was having with my Twin Flame. I said, "I know it's not right. It's like my karmic has projected all her love and relationship fears, worries, and anxiety and thrust it all upon you. And you're like the sacrificial lamb. You haven't done anything wrong, and I know it's not fair. I practically cried to her, 'I know it's not fair!'

And then, from my DM in the 5-D (or dreamspace), there followed a suggestion or an insinuation that I had betrayed her. I don't remember the exact words, but I clearly remember the accusation coming through. I pleaded with her…"I never betrayed you. I would NEVER betray you!"

I wanted her to hear me. I wanted these statements to pierce the veil and punch right through to where she could hear them while she was sleeping, where it would be such a powerful message, she would and could recall all of it upon waking the next morning. And then she may be able to forgive me for not shielding her more throughout the Journey, while we were in communications. Then she may be able to forgive me for not protecting her more, for not standing up more to my karmic when she said things like this (and for not being more loyal).

If—only if—I had known what the heck was going on, and what this Journey was. If, and only if, my Twin were open and receptive to receiving my 5-D apology. If—and only if—she hadn't had too much to drink the night before and it could come through (indulgements in alcohol seemed to have haunted us both a bit throughout our lives). Would she hear it? Would she ever hear it from me? Or was I just howling in the (night) wind?

I woke up and jotted some notes down in my iPhone notes app, and there that note has been sitting for months now. I didn't know what to do with it. Perhaps I just wanted to ruminate on it on a while.

And then tonight, in the shower, it came to me, I was (am) supposed to share it. Because something tells me that this concept of our Beloveds being mistreated by society by all the circumstantial dust the Twin Flame Journey "kicks up," isn't unique to just me and us. It seems to be a human thing. When and where humans take all their anxieties, fears, worries, doubts, and ego machinations related to whatever (in this case, love and relationships and sex and everything that comes with it) and put them onto someone else. When we project like this, though, it doesn't work. It means we've now (seemingly) distanced ourselves from the issue, we've separated ourselves from it (whatever it is), we've cut it (or them) off, and therefore, it doesn't exist anymore. WRONG! All we've done, rather than looking honestly at the truth and dealing with it, is push all our stuff onto another unsuspecting human. We've dumped our garbage right onto them. And that's a pretty (pardon the term) crappy thing to do.

Why do we do that? If I were a scholar of Freud or Jung, I'd probably know. [I am sure many of you readers do know.] That's not really my focus here, though, to get into pop psychology or what-not, but IT IS my focus to tell the truth and to help you all on your respective journeys.

Outside of the Twin Flame Journey, how many times in life did we isolate someone, cut them off, tell stories about them, try to taint others' opinions of them? Didn't we do it in the schoolyard, and at work, and in our social circles? Don't we do it today when we gossip?

Oh, "Look at her!" "What's she doing now?" "Did you see how she just looked at him (or her)?" "Did you see them together?" "You just know they are sneaking around, getting it on." "Do you think 'so-and-so' knows?" "What do their kids think?" "Oh, how horrible!" "What a despicable thing to do."

In our case, despite the "Homewrecker" moniker, we hadn't DONE anything, per se. We had met (er, ignited) on the 22nd of a beautiful summer month and experienced this tremendous spark, this unspeakable connection. The similarities were uncanny (and this is just a few of them): We shared the same Zodiac sign, we do similar things for a job, we do the same things for hobbies—art, writing, photography, we wear the same shoe size, we have the same hair color (typically), and we value independence, joy, and lightness (above most everything).

In full disclosure, in the physical space, we did give each other a quick kiss on the lips a handful of times, but it never really went beyond that for various, complex reasons (not the least of which was my own personal "standards" or belief system), not to mention my overwhelming sense of guilt because of my karmic partner and our kids and of course, the "prying eyes" and intense focus on our every move (when we were in public). People would watch and stare as she would fix my collar. Or as we spent more time together, my karmic would say, "Stay away from her; she's DANGEROUS!" or, "It's obvious just watching you two!"

Yes, I agree there is some impossible-to-understand and hard-(if-not-impossible)-to-believe super-cosmic power to this relationship that I will never understand, and that it all may never be totally balanced out and realized in this lifetime. But I have to remind myself that "Oh, it might!" and there's always room for a miracle. It happens. I know they do. I've seen them firsthand.

But in the meantime, I just wanted us as a Collective to recognize that our Divine Counterpart needs our compassion and loyalty to get through what society is going to—and is most likely currently—slinging at them as we navigate this Journey. Looking back, I wish I had been more loyal and taken a stronger stand, and I do now. I won't let anyone disparage her. I say, "Please. She has a first and a last name and deserves for them to be used." That power, that strength and that stance is new, and it feels good. I wish I'd had it earlier, but that is what this Journey is about, opening our eyes, elevating people, things, relationships, raising ourselves, achieving more Soul Growth and more integrity, and of course, following our purpose. And hopefully, one day, we'll be able to do that together as a Twin Flame (power) couple in Union. But if not, in the meantime, I've got her back and I hope she has mine. Let's all have each others' backs, too. This Journey is contrary to everything society has created and prescribed and it's never going to be an easy ride. But, we're all in this together. The reminder is that more compassion is needed and required for each and every human being on this Journey and those who are watching it unfold.

Your New "Double Life"

If you are on the Twin Flame Journey, and you have a karmic partner, a spouse, or a domestic partner, then most likely, you're having to lead something along the lines of a "double life." While everything in your body is programmed to resist this duality, you may find it's necessary to protect yourself while you figure out what's going on. First of all, the Twin Flame Journey seems surreal and it may take a very long while to make heads or tails of what's going on. Let's be clear: This isn't your typical 3-D story of person meets person in the workplace or at a social gathering, sparks ensue, and they start an affair (though some of you may have had that, or a similar experience in your Journey). It goes far beyond that and into a "soul level" connection that you cannot deny.

It's important that you protect yourself until you find your "footing," and in many ways, that can feel like you're being dishonest, or leading a double life.

Especially because the Journey seems so far-fetched and difficult—if not impossible—to explain to a spouse, a domestic partner, or a parent, son or daughter, or family member. Also, you don't want to run the risk of sounding "crazy" or "unhinged." To the uninitiated, this Journey will sound exactly like that.

I remember one night I was having drinks with my sorority sisters at a wedding, and things got quiet at the end of the evening and we were talking about "soul mates." I had had a few drinks and touched on the subject of "Twin Flames" just to test the water and to see if anyone knew what I was talking about. I followed up with, "You know, like soulmates, just 1,000 times stronger." Everyone looked at me like I had three eyeballs, so I quickly changed the subject. That was the first and last time I talked about Twin Flames in a social setting among the uninitiated!

Because this "relationship" (or perhaps a better term is "connection") is one that is divinely orchestrated and blessed, it's probably best to remain quiet until you have a good handle on your personal situation, especially if there is change involved, such as a separation or divorce (and especially if there are children involved). These relationships, if they can be called that, do not operate in the usual 3-D manner that we've all grown accustomed to. They are extremely rare, extremely extraordinary, and you must treat them delicately, and protect both you and your Divine Counterpart to the largest extent possible.

Sometimes, however, a lot of things may happen BEFORE you know this person is your Twin Flame. Don't beat yourself up. Be gentle on yourself. Be as authentic and as transparent as you can, within reason, with your spouse or domestic partner. But you should also, if possible, try to protect your Twin Flame, from judgment, from gossip, and exclusion from social groups. It's easy to do this when you know what's going on. It's more difficult to make reparations in hindsight after the damage is done. These are all very real dynamics on this Journey.

Many people call the "puppy love" phase of the Twin Flame relationship the "love bubble" phase. This will be when you've first met your Twin, and you're spending a great deal of time together. He or she will make you feel joyful, they will make you laugh, they will likely make you feel like you never have before (or at least, he or she will stir feelings that you haven't felt in what seems to be forever.) For me and my Twin, the feeling I can best recall is overflowing joy. When you are together and even in a group of people, you will feel like there is no one else around. It's like time stands still and a moment can last forever. (In fact, you want it to last forever.)

We would crack jokes and everyone else would just kind of look at us. She would make up nicknames for me, smooth my collar, adjust my shirt, just do little intimate things like a spouse or long-term partner would do. I would do the same for her. I went out of my way to care for her and to give her everything she needed while she was around me. When we would end up on a call or a FaceTime call, I would grin from ear to ear. The closest way I can describe it is like when you fall in love for the first time. It's like you cannot see anyone else, no one else exists for you. The love is pure, and it takes you over completely. You don't know why, but you love this person unconditionally (and sometimes in a very short amount of time). Time is compressed. Things move much more quickly than normal. The feelings come on fast and strong. And they're undeniable (at least, usually for the Twin who awakens first). The "awakened" Twin cannot deny the feeling.

Sometimes the other Twin will deny the feeling. Sometimes, he or she will be closed off to feeling such bliss. Perhaps his or heart isn't awakened as fully as the first Twin who recognizes the power of this love first. There are countless different scenarios, based on my experience and research, but there are some common denominators, too. And you can put faith in those common denominators.

The Worst Heartbreak
You've Ever Experienced

Being on the Twin Flame Journey is not for the faint of heart. Imagine the greatest love you've ever known, then imagine that love being taken from you time and time again. Imagine virtually the worst loss of your life, and then that gets re-enacted over and over again like a scene from the movie "Groundhog Day" every time you go through a physical or emotional Separation.

Imagine the worst comment someone has made to you in your life that stabbed you deep into the heart and then magnify that by 1,000. Imagine all you want to do is see and be with your Beloved, and seemingly, there are walls all around you and all around your Twin, too. Walls that are thousands of feet high and seemingly impossible to penetrate.

This is what Twin Flame heartbreak looks and feels like. In fact, it hurts so bad, it's difficult to put into words. When my Twin and I physically separated, I felt the greatest sense of palpable loss and sadness I had ever felt. I was in a depression or a state of despair for months. Being in the same places where we had been together, laughing, having fun, just feeling that special spirit connection, I just felt so lost, lonely, and isolated. I didn't know what was happening. But I realized and recognized the depths of the sadness and was very conscious that I had never quite felt anything like that before, for anyone, EVER.

And then there are the feelings of missing someone so deeply that you feel like you could just die. Luckily, I was able to learn how to transmute this feeling of loss and missing someone and replace it with the golden light of unconditional love and radiate that out to my Beloved. That is the only thing that can give me comfort when this feeling of separation and loss washes over me. It really is a matter of mastering and controlling your own thoughts. The only thing I can compare it to is when a child is misbehaving, redirecting that child to a more productive, fruitful, and pleasing activity. On the next page, I give you the four simple steps to transmute the feeling of loss and missing your Beloved.

How to Transmute the Feeling of Loss and Turn it Into a Message of Love Instead

1) Sit with the feeling of loss, of missing your Twin.

2) Take a few deep, healing breaths.

3) Meditate/concentrate on the good things about yourself and the love you feel for yourself.

4) Start imagining and shift to the intense feeling of love you have for your Divine Counterpart.

5) Play with that energy for a few minutes, and then send the energy outward to your intended Beloved.

It's that simple!

Blocks to Union

There are many blocks to Union that will arise along the way. You'll be going right along, moving and grooving, and then bam! You hit a brick wall and you wonder why.

If you dig around at the root of the trouble or the issue and if you're really honest with yourself, you'll discover the blocks within yourself that may be holding you back.

This can be things like feelings of low self-esteem, lack of self-worth, fear of abandonment, issues with family (mother, father, siblings, etc.), guilt, shame, fear of failure, fear of the future, fear of actually succeeding (!)

I recently had a quantum healing session with a wonderful and very experienced healer (Sylvia Escalante/TF Enchantress) and one of the messages that came through very strongly was that many of us Twins do not feel we are worthy of such a "big love." We feel we aren't ready for that, or that we're not capable of giving or receiving true, unconditional love. We may even feel we don't deserve it (even if we won't—or can't—admit this fact to ourselves). The vastness, the enormity of pure, unconditional love, the unknown of it scares many of us (this may even be a deeply hidden fear that you aren't even aware of).

Look deep within yourself. Examine your true feelings around love. Did your prior relationships taint your view of love? Did you feel abandoned, tricked, or betrayed by someone you loved? Did someone take advantage of you? Did many take advantage of you, or use you? Were you used for sex, for money, for stability, as a provider? Were you used as a crutch for someone else? Do (or did) you use love as a weapon? Do (or did) you use sex as a weapon? As a control mechanism? Did someone try to control you? Manipulate you? Suppress you?

Did you choose to be alone, rather than to risk conflict or rejection or abuse?

Did your parents (either one or both) abandon you? Did you feel alone, unwanted?

All of these very real, 3-D scenarios represent a twisted, distorted sort of love and is primarily the kind of love that the world we know has become accustomed to. In fact, you become so accustomed to it, that you feel like it's the real thing. It's the right—and only—thing. It's the "best you can do." But those are all lies. It's all you learn to accept. You learn not to ask for more, for fear of being disappointed time and again. So you settle for "fake love" and it keeps you from experiencing, receiving, and expressing real love.

In fact, you probably didn't know real love like this existed until you happened upon your Journey, right? I know I didn't. But I didn't realize it..."I didn't know what I didn't know."

It's time to acknowledge, clear, and purge those blocks, those false beliefs and lies, and to move into a brighter, higher, better state of being. It's possible. But you cannot do it if you aren't aware or don't acknowledge that these blocks or issues are present. Awareness and acknowledgement is the first step.

But the best part is healing these blocks. It may not feel good while you are healing them, but you will feel better—much better—after.

There are many ways to heal and this is just a short list of suggestions:

1) Meditation and breathwork. It's great to do this daily or as often as you can. I usually do a 20- or 22-minute meditation, but you can set your timer on your phone to do a session as long, or as short as you would like. There are also countless great guided meditations online, on YouTube. Look for those that have a lot of followers and "likes."

2) Prayer. Prayer is a powerful healer and the message has recently come to me that prayer is vastly underutilized. "Ask and ye shall receive." It's true. Our guides are constantly listening to us and responding. We are in a constant dialogue with them, a constant "feedback" loop if we only tune in and listen and speak our needs and wishes.

3) A certified Reiki healer (this is an ancient Japanese healing modality and sessions are generally very affordable). This serves to address energetic issues, remove energy blockages, and rebalance your chakras. Check out https://www.reiki.org/ for a healer near you.

4) Positive affirmations. Watch your thinking patterns. Try to change negative statements into positive ones. (Example: "I never get what I want" to "I often get what I want, and some recent examples are..." In this way you are re-programming your mind to think and express itself in more positive ways and this enables you to see more opportunity and less challenge and lack.)

5) Crystals. I am relatively new to using crystals and have only started to tap into their potential. There are many educational videos online. Buy stones that resonate with you, then use them during your daily meditations.

6) Tai chi (movement) or yoga. These disciplines will help in so many ways, from focus to physical and spiritual alignment, health and healing, and even including energy re-balancing.

7) Creating art and/or journaling. Expressing yourself is wonderful way to tap into your core issues and wounds and facilitate healing. You can do this with visuals and through your words. Both are very healing practices and it's great to make them a daily discipline, if you can.

8) Spending time in nature. Being in nature is a very healing activity, as it helps you ground your energies into the Earth and it helps open you to possibilities. (Try walking barefoot. Go into the forest. Sit outside in a quiet space. Maybe even consider meditating outside). By observing and listening to our animal and plant "friends," we can learn many insights and be taught many valuable lessons that are useful to us on our Journeys. Sometimes, too, the messages you receive will be just what you need to hear.

The best news is that, through this Journey, you have a new chance at love, a new opportunity with unconditional love, a bigger, better, richer, and more fulfilling love than you've ever experienced before. So, maybe it's time to put down your defenses, open your heart to this Journey and to everything it has to teach you. God/The Universe/Source Energy has put this at your feet. It seems to me that if you don't examine it, if you don't give it a try, well, then you'll never know. Isn't it better to try, than to never try at all?

The Importance of Surrender

"Always say 'yes' to the present moment...Surrender to what is. Say 'yes' to life – and see how life starts suddenly to start working for you rather than against you." – Eckhart Tolle

There are so many important stages of the Twin Flame Journey, but the stage of surrender is among the hardest steps, but the most important.

Only when we've knocked our ego down to size until it's barely noticeable, transmuted our "negative" emotions, such as fear and doubt, and then placed our trust in God, the Goddess, the Universe, Mother Gaia, your guides, your ancestors, or whomever you believe is your higher power, can you fall to your knees and turn it all over to "them." In fact, I've turned it over to them over and over again. (Many times.) It is at the point where you turn control over that you actually release yourself from bondage. (And you may have to release yourself over and over again, or watch carefully and closely to make sure old patterns are not re-emerging.)

I am not in Union with my Beloved Divine Counterpart, my beautiful Twin Flame yet, but I can tell you the process of surrender has been so valuable to me and I actually cherish the ability to relinquish control and let something larger than myself guide and direct the path of my little boat, sailing on this sea of unconditional love.

When Your Love Isn't Reciprocated in the "Real World"...A Reality of Being on the Journey

This twisty, turn-y Journey, the Twin Flame Journey has its ups and downs and anyone on the Journey knows this is true.

Perhaps one of the most disappointing recent setbacks for me was when I finally put my karmic partner of 20 years in her proper place (meaning, I stood in my own authority and let her know I was a sovereign being deserving of respect) and releasing myself from the bondage of that situation. Once free, I suppose I had this subconscious thought in the back of my mind that that would be it. A switch would flip and I'd be magically on my way to Re-Union or Union with my Divine Counterpart, my beloved Twin Flame. Maybe it would be instantaneous.

Not so fast.

(Says the Universe/Source Energy).

I've been working on Patient Endurance for almost three years now. I've done the work consistently, managing the triggers, the clearings, the purgings, the meditations, the Violet Flame (you can look that up if you haven't heard of it), following every synchronicity and being grateful for them and the entire Journey. I was pretty sure I was earning an "A+". But unlike the "real world," this Journey isn't judged with grades, a progress meter, or an indicator light.

I then got hit with another proverbial brick wall recently. I was flying high and all signs (in the 5-D) seemed like they were pointing to Union. All the readers were saying it. The energies are high. My guides were pushing me forward, encouraging me to "go for it." My dreams in the 5-D were "off the chain." Wonderful, positive dreams, full of unconditional love, hugs, and canoodling freely with my Divine Masculine with no obstacles or interruptions. A clear path to Nirvana.

But then I followed my guides and made my approach to my Twin once again in the 3-D. I had meditated on the perfect way to make contact again and to get my Divine Counterpart "to dance with me" (so to speak, to participate in the 3-D). It seemed perfect.

But again, not so fast.

After I dropped off a very thoughtful and immaculately wrapped gift (at least, in terms of my wrapping abilities, it was about as perfect as you could get). It was in our "signature color" of gold, a color that has resonance for us in this Journey (as well as a note identifying myself … finally … as the mysterious gifter of gifts over the past three months)…it had been a trio of perfect gifts, hand-picked for my Divine Counterpart. This one was the last in the series, the "big reveal." I hadn't spent much, but the gifts were all thoughtful. Things I thought that she would love.

Well, the response was fairly immediate (in terms of our usual snail's pace of timing). Within a few hours, I received a response note. I am largely paraphrasing, but the gist of it…"Thanks for the gifts. It wasn't necessary. Please stop gifting. It makes me feel uncomfortable and I have (essentially) disconnected myself from you after the toxic events between [INSERT NAMES HERE TO PROTECT THE INNOCENT AND THE LIKELY NOT-SO-INNOCENT.] I don't feel the same about you as you do me. In fact, I have a serious new relationship and I am moving out of state. I wish you the best."

This is the third time I have been rejected on this Journey, and every time has been as blunt and as brutal as I am describing above. However, I had prepared myself for this eventuality and tried to neutralize my emotions about it, recognizing that the response that came—whether good or bad—would still arrive, chock-full of lessons, just like all the others. This rejection was more difficult, though, because I had purposely given the gifts with the intention that they be received in the spirit of "unconditional love," "with no expectations." I had learned my lessons of release and SURRENDER. So, I felt I had the perfect ingredients to a successful outcome.

Turns out, that was wrong (at least, for now, it appears so). This experience has taught me that the 5-D and the 3-D may not be aligned, yet (even if you are feeling it is so). Meaning, if you're experiencing something in the 5-D, it doesn't appear to automatically translate to the 3-D. I was testing an assumption and it proved to be wrong. It also appears by all accounts that this "experiment" with the Journey was a colossal failure. But I keep trying to remind myself that many readers and even my guides will say, "Trust your intuition," and "There's far more going on than one can see on the surface" and also that, "Sometimes you may be making progress when you don't realize it, or cannot see it."

But this is difficult to acknowledge today, under the light of a new day, when it appears that all I have is a case of possible unrequited love, a love interest that is riding off into the sunset with someone else, and an overactive imagination. That is what my rational brain says to me. But my heart still sees it differently. But that same beating, bloody, bruised heart is more quiet today, more shy, more reticent. It's not beating its chest today about "this big love." My heart today, is mostly hanging its head, a sad shadow of its prior self. Yep, my heart took a beating again. My body and spirit took its third body blow. A total knockout. And not in a good way.

So, now, I must find a way to get back to that "high vibe" state I normally am on.

IF...if...if...it is unrequited love, I am still grateful for this twisty-turny Journey and everything it's taught me about self-love, self-worth, confidence, and most of all, perfect, unconditional love. I am still the vessel of perfect love that I sought to be. I still love her with all my heart. And in that, I am still victorious.

Even in Separation,
We are Co-Creating

The long road to Twin Flame re-Union/Union is a twisty-turny Journey, tiring, and lonely (at times), with lots of challenges and opportunity. In periods of Separation, or long Separation (years or many years), it is easy to feel lost, alone, distressed, betrayed by both your Twin and the Universe (even though that is all an illusion).

It's important to remember that despite all the hurt you are experiencing, that even in this stage of the Twin Flame Journey, that you and your Beloved are still co-creating. Prior to incarnating into the 3-D, you both designed this experience for both of you. So that each of you could experience any "triggers," clear those triggers, and then transmute them, and in the end, overcome them.

So, when you're angry at your Twin, or angry at the Universe/Source energy, please just remember that this was your own Journey, designed by you and your Twin, for the highest and greatest soul evolution of each of your souls. There are many lessons buried deep within the Journey that must be unearthed, examined, dusted off, cleaned, and then put in their proper places.

It's all part of the Journey. At every turn, one should ask themselves, "What lesson is intended in this [moment, event, occurrence]? What am I supposed to learn, absorb, and integrate into my being?"

Remember: This 3-D experience is all a simulation (of sorts). The good stuff is on the other side, just waiting for us to meet it.

There are also some other important things to remember (all things I learned along the way) on this Journey:

1) **We are never alone.** You will feel alone and lonely and it's important to remember that all is just an illusion. You have your Twin, as well as an army of Divine support, behind you, every step of the way. In the immortal words of the band, Journey (it's ironic now that they've long been one of my favorite bands with the name "Journey"), "don't stop believin'" and keep the faith. You cannot see your divine guides, but you can feel them. And you can hear them. They will sound like your own intuition. They are talking to you every minute of every day. And, you are divinely guarded

and protected. In fact, we are more aided and protected than we can know or realize. Follow your gut instincts, follow your hunches, listen to the higher voice(s) that you hear, the voice of truth. It's your internal compass. Don't dismiss it. It's there for a reason.

2) **You are not simply an individual any more.** You are part of a pair. Part of an eternal, immortal, and Divine pair. Further, you are part of a Collective now. A collective of either Divine Feminines or Divine Masculines, each a strong and wondrous Army advancing, anchoring, and unleashing unconditional love on the planet. And for that role, you must remain strong even when you feel weak and faithful when you feel hopeless. You are not alone. You are on the front lines, along with all of us, and it's important that no woman or man be left behind. So look to your left, look to your right, see who's struggling on the Journey, and who needs your help (no matter how small the help). Pick them up and put them on your back like Saving Private Ryan and help carry them there with us. We're all in this together.

3) **When you work to heal yourself, you are also healing your Twin, and by extension, the Collective.** Anytime you do clearing work or energy work on yourself or have someone else

facilitate it for you (this would be things such as a massage, reiki, crystal healing, therapy with a like-minded individual, talking it out with a friend from the Twin community, a past life regression, an inner child healing, a guided healing meditation on YouTube, or meditations in general, just to name a few examples), you are not only healing your core wounds and issues, you are also healing your Twin. You may not realize it, but even doing small amounts of self-work and self-care can ripple outward like a pebble in a pond in wonderful and unexpected ways. A little goes a long way. Take care of you. Taking care of you takes care of your Twin and the Collective, too. That will then flow outward to everyone you interact with, and from there it flows outward still. It's a win-win-win-win-win …

On Miracles, Manifestations, Synchronicities, and the Mysterious Red Thread

To be on the Twin Flame Journey means you will become more and more comfortable with not only synchronicities, which will become an everyday occurrence (sometimes occurring hundreds of times a day), but that you will also become more comfortable with manifestations that will often feel like a miracle. Since I started the Journey, I have encountered approximately 30 instances of miracles or uncanny/ freakish timing and inexplicable coincidences. One can put them all into the "miracles" category, or the more skeptical may categorize them into a few different buckets. But...and I can assure you that this is true, there will be miracles like "the red thread" for many of you that will keep you going even when all seems hopeless. But more on the red thread in a few minutes after we talk about these other incredible and unbelievable occurrences.

If you've been on the Journey for any length of time, you have no doubt experienced synchronicities that you associate with your Divine Counterpart, your Twin Flame. These will be things like numbers, number combinations, songs, animals, birds, insects, colors, and your Twin's name or initials. You will begin to see them everywhere, once you are aware you have a Twin. They will be on signs, on license plates, on billboards, on TV and in movies, in songs, in comments people make to you, in phrases that have some significance to you and your Twin, and they will come countless times a day, sometimes in the hundreds.

On one occasion, a symbol that I had identified and correlated to my Twin occurred to me 39 times in a single two-hour span. It will seem crazy to you. It will be something that you particularly don't want to share with anyone, unless you have a friend or close friend who is also going through the Journey, or if you have spiritually evolved friends who won't laugh or make fun of you, or minimize when you share these happenings that are beyond coincidence.

(Separate note: Be careful who you share with before you share, as there can be "negative" blowback or feedback that comes to you that is not true. The "average" human being having an "average" 3-D existence consisting of

birth, school, work, bills, and then deaths cannot even begin to fathom the amazing creativity and playfulness of the Universe and of Source Energy. And he or she may say things to you like, "That's crazy." Or, "Are you sure you're not just obsessing?" Or they will secretly think to himself or herself that you are becoming obsessive, possibly even exhibiting some traits or characteristics similar to "stalking." The "average" human mind will go there and try to make sense of what cannot make sense, unless you know.

Unless you've started the Journey, or you are on the Journey, you can most likely never understand or begin to comprehend all of this. (So, if you are one of those people who think this sounds crazy, then you can stop reading now, because this information is not intended for you. Please, with all due respect, we love you, but please move along.)

Along your Journey, there will be timing coincidences, like something out of a movie. There will be repeating karma incidences (think "Groundhog Day") … until you clear the karma by making a different decision. Until you make a different choice, you will be stuck in a feedback loop and everything will remain the same, as it always has. Once you make the conscious decision to make a different choice, everything will open up to you and that is when miracles will happen.

For example, as I and a friend were examining our journeys, certain facts came up that were indisputable for each of us, respective to our own journeys. I will only speak to my own Journey, but there seemed to be cycles as to when things would happen. Like if my Twin and I went into Separation, it would be on a specific date, and then we would come out of Separation, and then we would go into Separation again, a year later, on that exact same date. That is just one example.

There was a point in time in my third year of the Journey, and after two Separation phases from my Twin in which I was getting very "down in the dumps" about the whole thing. I was filled with a ton of doubt and wracked with worry and fear. I began to question myself: "We've both incarnated on this planet in this lifetime. Surely, there is a reason for that and we are meant to come into Union to reunite and also to fulfill our Soul Purpose and mission."

At this point in time, across about a three-week span, I mysteriously found a red thread just while I was going about my daily routine. The first time, it was a teeny-tiny thread on a couch.

Then, a week later, it was a thread in front of me as I was walking behind a car after food shopping, a thread that stretched from the car's left-hand side to its right-hand side, coming out of a trunk. The third time was a longer red thread, found in my front yard.

Then, some more time passed, I found a twisty, turny, loopy red thread in one of our garden beds in the back yard as I was cleaning up the yard. Then about a week later, I found one on the floor of my family's business, a beautiful and intact red thread. So, all told, I have now found six threads in total. Some friends of mine on the Journey have independently stated that they have found threads, too. In fact, I did an informal poll and more self-identifying Twins had received or experienced a red thread than had not (at a ratio of 6 receiving a red thread to 1 not receiving). If that's not tangible proof of a miracle or many miracles, I am not sure what else is. What are the odds? All I know is, looking at my red threads (I've kept some of them) gives me that tangible proof that this Journey is real and that Divine Intervention is at play.

What is the Symbolism of the Red Thread?

First, let's talk about the meanings associated with the color red. According to the book, "The New Secret Language of Symbols: An Illustrated Key to Unlocking Their Deep and Hidden Meanings" by David Fontana, red is the color of good fortune, celebration, and weddings, and it is the first of the five colors of Chinese cosmology.

Red also represents chi and it is the color of summer and the element of fire. It has long been used by royals and the church, and it also is seen as the luckiest of all colors. It has the inherent ability to ward off negative energy. It also symbolizes the sun, the heavens, light, gold, and even prosperity.

Red is also associated with yang and longevity and was used by ancient alchemists who were seeking to make an elixir for eternal life. In today's world, it is associated with all things love: Valentine's Day, the color of a representative heart-shape, and Cupid. So, in short, the color red has a lot going for it.

Now what about the red thread? What's up with that?

According to Wikipedia (my kids have asked me never to cite Wikipedia, but I learned well from them, so I am not listening...side note: Please make a donation to Wikipedia if you can):

> The **Red Thread of Fate** (<u>simplified Chinese</u>; <u>traditional Chinese</u>; <u>pinyin</u>: *Yīnyuán hóngxiàn*), also referred to as the **Red Thread of Marriage**, and other variants, is an <u>East Asian</u> belief originating from <u>Chinese legend.</u> According to this myth, the gods tie an invisible red cord around the ankles of those that are destined to meet one another in a certain situation or help each other in a certain way. Often, in Japanese and Korean culture, it is thought to be tied around the <u>little finger</u>. According to Chinese legend, the deity in charge of "the red thread" is believed to be *<u>Yuè Xià Lǎorén</u>*, often abbreviated to *Yuè Lǎo*, the old lunar matchmaker god, who is in charge of marriages.

The two people connected by the red thread are destined lovers, regardless of place, time, or circumstances. This magical cord may stretch or tangle, but never break. This myth is similar to the Western concept of <u>soulmate</u> or a destined flame.

The red thread is also tied to the Jewish Kabbalah, a mystical belief system and a red thread is tied around your left wrist to offer you protection against negative energy (or in the olden days, as it was called, "the evil eye.") This is consistent with the ongoing assertion from Archangel Michael and our spirit guides to all Twin Flames that you are protected throughout your Journey. If you listen to readers on YouTube, you'll hear this asserted many times. I choose to believe it.

Once I found my first red thread, I didn't give it much thought. That is, until I found one, and then another, and another, in succession.

What this did, except starting a new red thread collection for me, was to give me something tangible to point to, to touch, to feel, when I began to doubt the Twin Flame relationship (if one can call it that...many dispute that term, but given that there is real back and forth, for the purposes of this guide, I am going to call it a relationship) and the Journey.

Further, I was very excited to learn that my best friend on this Twin Flame Journey, someone who is in a Twin Flame relationship herself, had also begun to find red threads also. She sat on one on a friend's couch, and then she found another and another. I think she is now "up" to 6 or 7 threads.

Bottom line to me on this is that I believe that finding the red threads is more than a coincidence, it represents nothing short of a miracle. A way for the higher world, or the heavens, or the angels, or whatever you believe is "Beyond" to communicate with us and show and share that this Twin Flame relationship or Journey is REAL. A real, tangible thing. Just as real as the table and the computer upon which I am writing this guide.

It may seem ethereal at times. It may seem untouchable at times. It may seem like your wildest imagination. Or a dream. Or a fairy tale. But the truth is, it's real. And you'll soon know, if you don't already. (Unless it's not ... but we'll get to that later.)

Not everyone is on a Twin Flame Journey, even though some desperately want to be. This is very different from soulmates, or the classic and traditional dream of 3-D love and happily ever after. That does exist. And one can find their happily-ever-after in this Twin Flame relationship, too. (But we'll also get to that later).

Two Little Birds

Along the rocky and yet rewarding path of your Journey, you will see signs and synchronicities that will have meaning for you. It could be a symbol, a number, a series of numbers, a song, or it could be animals or insects (my Twin and I have particular resonance with the Monarch butterfly, the symbol of transformation, beauty and freedom). You'll need to pay attention to all the signs and synchronicities along the way and use your intuition (or Google) to decipher what these synchronicities and symbols mean for you and your Twin.

So many interesting and unusual things have happened on my Journey and I wanted to share with you at least one of those incidences.

One of the things I really enjoy doing in my spare time is spending time by my pool. Around the pool there is a pool cage (as is customary where I live) that screens in the pool and keeps out animals, amphibians, and insects. Because I have a cat and a couple of dogs, however, we keep the pool cage doors cracked ever so slightly so that our pets can easily walk in and out of the cage and into our fenced yard.

One day, I was working out by the pool, and two little brown birds had made their way inside the cage. I thought to myself, having had prior experience with birds being where they're not supposed to be (one once got into my house!)...so I grabbed my pool net and had resigned myself to the fact that I was going to have to carefully capture them with the net and then release them outside of the cage. Much to my surprise, they quickly and efficiently flew across the entire cage's span and out the other slightly open door, one following the other. I thought to myself, "Wow, they found the opening! Just look at them go."

I told a friend about this (who is also on the Journey), and she remarked that it is highly unusual for birds to be able to find their way out of anything (which were my sentiments exactly). There were two little birds, not apart, but together, and they found the opening. I likened this to my Twin Flame Journey and took it as a sign that even when you're not sure the two of you will be able to find "the opening" or the way to come together in Union again, that you *will* find a way, someday. Seeing these two little birds filled me with so much hope and possibility.

Fast forward, months later, as I am still going about my Journey of soul evolution and soul growth. Much had happened, but the two birds (my Twin and I, metaphorically speaking) still hadn't found "our opening." By this point, I had reached a point of self-satisfaction and contentment and didn't even need to find the opening anymore, or the need or drive to reach Union quite so much. I was fairly neutral on that point, even though I still care(d) about my Twin greatly and had surrendered to whatever Life/the Universe/God/Source Energy was going to throw at me. Either way, I knew I would be fine.

I was standing in my dining room, by a large picture window. I think I was getting ready to sit down and eat lunch. Lo and behold, what do you know, that little brown bird had swooped in and landed on the patio table inside the cage and in front of me AGAIN. He (or she) just looked at me. Then the bird did a little hop dance around the table. Again, I had the same thought...that I was going to have to help the little bird escape the cage.

Just as I was thinking that, the second bird flew in and joined the other bird on the table. They did a little tit-a-tat dance together, very obviously in front of me, like they were trying to make a point. Then, together, they flew right out the other door again. And I had the same thought again...that "Wow, they've found the opening together again." Not once, but twice, those two little birds found their way out (and up). Those birds have given me so much hope, just like the red thread.

I do believe that nature and the Universe are trying to interact with us daily, to show us things that will resonate, to make a point, to help us understand where we are on our Journey, or simply, to give us hope along the way.

Faith

There is one thing you need to know about this Journey (aside from the fact, that at its essence, it is about unconditional love) and it is: To be on this Journey means you MUST have faith.

This message came to me one very hot afternoon, along with the urging insistence that this topic must be included in this guidebook. This "faith" we are talking about IS the faith that one would associate with the most fervent Christian (or other) ideology. Just as the Bible talks about faith...

So do not fear, for I am with you; do not be dismayed, for I am your God. I will strengthen you and help you; I will uphold you with my righteous right hand.

— Isaiah 41:10 (NIV)

During this Journey, you can be assured that whatever/ whichever God you pray to, or whatever your belief, that you're not walking on your Journey alone. God/ Jesus/Buddha/Universe/Source Energy and/or your spirit guides are always right there with you, just as they have always been. There are times, particularly in Separation, where you will feel abandoned, neglected, and to use another Biblical term "forlorn." You will, at times, feel utterly alone. But just as you are feeling that feeling, you can be assured that if you tune in to your heart, you'll feel the help, the divine guidance that is right there beside you, if you only ask.

Two of the messages that kept coming through to me along the Journey that may be helpful to you is that: "This love is written in the stars." (Meaning your love with your Twin is divinely orchestrated and protected.)

AND...

"If God wills it, there is nothing (and I mean NOTHING) that will stand in its way." (If that doesn't give you confidence, I don't know what will.)

When I got low (and I mean at times, really, really low), you must remember to invoke your faith (whatever it is, in anything that is larger than yourself) and call to it. Ask for help. Pray. Ask for guidance. Ask for insights that you can easily understand. And you will be answered.

Also, it's important to remember to keep your beacon of love, your lighthouse, shining bright, for your Divine Partner. It is imperative that you love him or her with a constant and consistent love, as much as possible. The outcome of the Journey depends on your level of commitment and your level of faith. Of course, you are human, so you will waver at times, but it's important to not waver for too long. Check out the playlist at the end of this book, as well as Twin Flame movies to help you return to a higher vibe state when you're feeling down.

Even when I was low on faith, there was still at least the one tangible thing I could point to, the collection that I now keep right here on my desk, those mysterious red threads that tell me there is something far more to this Journey than meets the eye. You may have a different symbol other than a red thread, maybe something meaningful that has come to you or has transpired as a result of the Journey. Cling to that thing. And to your faith. And never let it go.

Patient Endurance

One of the other biggest lessons of the entire Journey and one that has perhaps been the hardest for me, because I am not a patient person, is the learning of patient endurance. The ability to wait, and wait, and wait some more. (And it's hard to judge the effectiveness of anything you do, particularly if you and your Twin are in Separation, which is very hard for many people.)

Patient endurance is particularly difficult for those of us who pounce on problems or issues, who work quickly to solve anything that comes up, and pride ourselves on making the most niggly situations work out perfectly through our well-timed thought process, dedication, effective and timing action and persistence. None of these things that have served us so well in the 3-D will serve you now. It's the truth. For now, throw that life experience and those tools out the window. They will be of no use to you now.

This Journey is about looking inward, reflecting, and problem-solving on yourself (because that is frankly, all you have control over). When you suspect your Twin is feeling fear, or if you receive an intuition about that, then work to address that feeling of fear in yourself in whatever way that now makes sense to you. What you do for yourself mirrors over to your Twin.

As a practical example to hopefully give life to this concept. In the case of fear...fear can relate to, or is associated with, both the root chakra and the sacral chakras. You can do a meditation or practice Reiki (or go to a session with a certified Reiki practitioner) to address that issue within your chakras and achieve more balance because balance is the goal.

Based on the concept of mirroring, which we explained in earlier pages, when you do this for yourself, you'll be helping not only yourself, but your Twin. In my experience, these are the types of actions that work best (and I am sure there are more) in reaching your desired outcomes, whether you're addressing fear or a lack of speaking your truth: Meditation or quiet contemplation, prayer, Reiki and/or other energetic healing modalities.

A good friend of mine says meditation just isn't for her, and she prefers the action and movement of yoga instead (but even in most yoga venues, there is quiet meditation at the end of the practice) which can be helpful. Some of my most valuable insights have come at the end of a yoga session!

About Karmic Cycles and Their Role in the Twin Flame Journey

One of the many dynamics of the Twin Flame relationship are karmic cycles. These karmic cycles are a particular situation, event, or occurrence that will keep repeating itself until you or your Twin Flame make a different choice, then the karmic cycle will end.

For example, my Twin and I have a repeating karmic cycle in that we go into Separation on the same specific day each year for two years in a row now. A friend of mine has a karmic cycle with her Twin that involves certain turns of events, such as a medical procedure and a request for one Twin to help another that also has repeated itself once a year, for two years. This time, both my friend and I are making different choices (than we originally did) when we are presented with the exact same circumstance in order to help the karmic cycle come to a close.

One may also say that when we are doing this, when we are making a different choice, that we are helping ourselves and our Twins move to a "higher timeline." What this means is that you then become elevated to a higher energy level, kind of like the way you "level up" in a video game. Then new lessons and learnings will present themselves, and then your souls will be able to advance into a higher state of being as you go along and make better, healthier choices that are in alignment with your Soul Purpose and Mission and that add to the greater and most highest good.

This is an important and critical part of the Twin Flame Journey, and even as I write this, my friend and I are co-collaborating on our learnings on the Journey, we are learning more and more about the cycles.

One thing to keep in mind is that, even in a Separation phase, you and your Twin are co-creating the circumstance, so being mad at him or her doesn't make any sense actually because you and he or she created this set of circumstances before you incarnated in order to help your soul grow and evolve and in order to help each of you ascend. You designed the challenges that you wanted presented to yourself and that is what you are co-creating along with your Twin.

So, for the same reason, even in Separation, it doesn't make sense to be mad at your Twin (even though that's a very real and natural emotion), because you and he or she embedded your Journey when it was originally planned with triggers and separations and the whole nine yards.

Just think about it: Would you have evolved had things remained easy, or the same? Would you have evolved if things had been happy-go-lucky the entire time you were interacting with your Twin? Would the two of you experience Soul Growth if you never had the opportunity to evolve? Would the two of you have grown or changed if there were never any "choppy waters" and only "smooth sailing?" Would the two of you ever be ready for Union if you didn't have the opportunity to heal the parts of yourselves that needed clearing and healing? Would you have been conscious of what needed to be cleared and healed had your Twin not "triggered" you?

Let's be real, however. We have these conversations with ourselves every day, too. Like, we go from being crazy in love with our Twin to mad as a hornet because they won't do or say what we want, or they won't act in the way that we wish. We can get spitting mad, but it just doesn't make sense to do that when you remember that this is a joint project. These lessons are all hard to deal with, and they hurt like hell as you are processing through them, but they are all part of the Journey. Your Journey. Your own customized, personalized Journey that was made **by** you and your Twin...**for** you and your Twin.

Why is This Twin Flame Journey so Difficult?

Think back to a time when you had a very challenging class and could not "get" a concept. Remember how your teacher or instructor had you working the same problem over and over again until you "got" it? In this same way, the Twin Flame Journey is designed like this.

The Twin Flame Journey is so difficult because it's a "school" for emotional and spiritual mastery. Our guides or the Universe or Source energy (whichever or whatever deity or spiritual guidance you lean on) has us repeat these "triggers," and learnings and lessons over and over again so that we may master them. This is of particular importance when we come into Union/Re-Union with our Twin. In this way, we are able to quickly and easily navigate future "triggers" from our partner so the Union can be as smooth and as successful as possible. Of course, once in Union, we will continue to learn and experience new lessons and new growth with our Divine Counterpart, but the intent is to make it much quicker to work through and resolve issues. Had we not gone through all the agony of the Journey and experienced painful lessons over and over again, we might be doomed to keep repeating them once we come back into Union with our Twin.

And if outdated, 3-D issues kept popping up, well, you can imagine how that would distract you from your Soul Purpose and Life Mission. It is this way ... beyond difficult ... by design. Isn't that brilliant?

Dealing with Doubt on the Journey (a.k.a. "When You Wanna Say, "Just Fuck It!")

Everyone deals with doubt and bouts of seeming (or real!) depression on the Journey ... everyone. You may not see the truth, connections or the patterns until some additional time passes. For example, things that didn't make sense to me many months ago now make complete sense to me. The puzzle pieces get filled in. They get filled in very, very slowly, but they get filled in. And then you can step back and see the full puzzle. You can see it for what it is.

If you're not yet communicating or in Union, it's possible that either one or the both of you have not yet learned your soul lessons that you set out to learn when you co-created/designed this Twin Flame Journey.

When you encounter any doubt or frustration or blocks, just remember: This is a co-creation between you and your Twin to trigger you in a certain way to elicit an emotion or a response as a test of faith.

When you let doubt creep into your mind (and believe you me, that has happened to me), try to turn it into a positive thought. We know that negativity will only prolong your path to reconnection and Union.

This Journey is one of faith and of acts. In the Bible, it says that faith without action is dead. So, have hope. Have faith. Believe. Act in alignment with your values. And see where that takes you

It's your prerogative. Every choice is yours to make.

Want to walk away from the Journey? Ok, then do that. But before you do that, to help you weigh it all out, I've come up with this handy-dandy little chart. Take a look-see. Maybe you'll agree. Maybe you'll disagree. My intent is to give you "food for thought."

Scenario 1 – Let's call this the "Blue Pill" *(in honor of the movie, The Matrix)…"The story ends, you wake up in your bed and believe whatever you want to believe."*	Outcomes	Cons, or Drawbacks
Abandon the Journey and try to return to normal, 3-D life	• Maybe make more money or do better in your career because you'll have more time to focus on work (this Journey can be distracting, as you well know!) • Maybe find a partner, a spouse • Still have thoughts of Twin Flame • Ability to look out for oneself (important)	• Miss out on the true love of your life • Have an "ordinary" life • Miss out on Soul Purpose/ Soul Mission • Leave your spiritual gifts on the shelf; "use it or lose it"

Scenario 2 – "Red Pill" *(in honor of the movie, The Matrix)…"You stay in Wonderland, and I show you how deep the rabbit hole goes."*	Outcomes	Cons, or Drawbacks
Keep going on the Journey; keep processing; keep clearing; keep transmuting; keep expressing, giving, and receiving love and unconditional love without expectation	• Create a new path that is in more (or total alignment) with your Soul Urge • Maybe receive a miracle • Maybe receive and join the love of your life • Maybe have a partner, spouse, family that is ideal for you • Still have thoughts of Twin Flame • Continue with the "bliss" part of the Journey • Ascend and personally evolve • Use your spiritual gifts	• Maybe have less money now because you are focused on others, your Soul Purpose and Soul Mission • Occasional bouts of doubt • Occasional bouts of emotion (which you experience anyway in 3-D life, so this one is actually cancelled out)

	• Help planet Earth and leave it better than you found it • Fulfill Soul Purpose/Soul Mission • Have faith and receive your spiritual reward • Envision and co-create your new, fantastic, amazing future	

Again, it's completely YOUR choice.

Are You Really Ready for Union?

When I was struggling with why my Twin had not reached out, why we were still not in communication, why things hadn't resolved, a very good and wise friend (who is also a Twin) said to me. "What if [NAME] just ran to you with open arms right this very minute. Would you be ready for that?"

I had to be honest with her and myself and say, "Actually, no." Because of the Journey and all the things that had happened along the way, there was a level of mistrust in the 3-D with my Twin. That was really a surprising answer coming from me, but the honest one. I wasn't ready. And I had mistrust. So, with that energy, I was still creating blocks that prolonged the Journey/Union, etc. I thought it was all her. Turned out it was me (or me, too).

That means there are more issues to be worked through, more emotions and baggage to purge, more truths to face, more things to acknowledge, and more things to grow past.

That, my friends, is called evolution or ascendance. And it appears maybe I'm still not ready. It's not all her. It's me, too.

When you are thinking that thing about your Twin (and pointing and blaming), as they say, there's a finger pointed at that person, but there are three more fingers pointing right back to yourself.

Things to be Grateful for on the Journey

This is a tough question, because there's so much to be grateful for on this Twin Flame Journey. I really had to dig deep to figure out a good answer to this.

First, I am grateful for the knowingness of how intricately connected our lives are to, not just to our Beloveds, but to the Divine. Seeing signs and synchronicities countless times a day just reminds me of all the unseen magic in the world that all too often, goes unnoticed. If everyone just knew what a huge safety net, what loving, magical bubble-wrap we have around ourselves at all times, I think the world would be a radically different place.

I now have a very close and intimate relationship with the Divine. We talk daily, sometimes many times a day. And we all thought God didn't talk to us anymore. Well, He/She does. Whether it's through the Archangels,

Romance Angels, or your spirit guides or ancestors, that trusted and proven guidance from Source is definitely coming through, loud and clear, like a best friend hanging on the phone with you until all hours, just listening to whatever you need and ask for.

The Twin Flame Journey brought me deeper into a greater understanding of not only the Divine, but of my own Soul and my own Self. It really helped to explain the history and the mysteries of my entire life. It gave me greater perspective so I could see and understand why things happened the way they did, both before the Journey and during the Journey. I suppose it gave me more of an ability to see things maybe the way God or the Angels see them, without judgment, and instead with loving, unconditional understanding of myself and everyone involved.

I now walk around the grocery store or just anyplace asking myself, "Could I be like Jesus, and love this person (as one person passes me by) and this person (as another passes me by) and this person (yes, even the ones who jump my place in line)?" I can now resoundingly say "Yes!" when I could never say that before. In fact, I would have never thought to ASK myself that question before.

The whole experience taught me there are no mistakes on this Journey. Things I thought I did "wrong" or did at the wrong time ... I learned that everything happened and happens for a reason, and everything unfolds in a certain way for a reason, in its own beautiful timing.

Honestly, the thing I most fought is having to be more patient than ever before. This is obviously not one of my strong suits, but I had to learn "Patient Endurance." When I felt myself getting impatient, I learned to remind myself, "All in Divine Timing." I had to give up my control issues. That was a tough one, and a challenge I still haven't mastered completely!

And above all, this Journey taught me Unconditional Love, and what that feels like, something I had never experienced before, other than with my parents and my two children. This is a love that will crack and burst your heart open with joy and make you want to sing from the hills about the love you have found, this love you hold so closely in your heart that it hurts in the most wonderful and profound way. And even when things get tough, the love is always there, burning with the consistency of a beating heart.

The Journey also brought me into alignment with myself, with my Beloved, and with the Divine. I can now easily feel when I am in alignment and when I am out of alignment. When I am feeling the flow of unconditional love and when I have become the perfect vessel for that perfect love, then I know it doesn't get any better than that for a human being. And though I don't currently hold that state continuously, I know how to get back to it when I get off track.

This Journey taught me to walk tall and proud and to be the Empress that I am. To embrace my God-given talents, skills, and abilities and to never hide or shield them. It brought out abilities that I had never discovered or knew I had before (such as claircognizance). It taught me that I am supposed to not hoard these abilities, but to share them with humanity and to spread them across a much wider group of people (beyond my own small family). I feel proud to be the Empress. That is beyond empowering and is also a great responsibility. I think there's an old quote, "With great gifts, comes great responsibility." And I am happy to do it!

And last, but certainly not least, this Journey brought you, my Beloved, a person, a soul who gave me so much while expressing so little as I've come to understand communications and intimacy. I quickly learned that I needed to stop forcing communications (or trying to) in the 3-D world, and it was like an epiphany to figure out: "Oh yeah, I can talk to her anytime I want, in the dream state, in the 5-D, using telepathy, sending her energy for healing and love." That was perhaps the most surprising discovery of all. That and the fact that we have so much more power than we ever imagined.

I am delighted that I found someone I love so much and who loves me, too, right back (even if not obvious or demonstrated in the 3-D right now). The perfect pair. In a soul-to-soul eternal embrace. I cannot wait for all of humanity to experience this love. Imagine how things will change.

Is Union Really the Point, Or Not?

If you spend any time online or on social media, it will appear that Union is the end-all-be-all, nirvanic reason for the whole Twin Flame Journey. And that is because we are thinking of this "relationship" in the 3-D sense, in the sense that we are used to.

But this isn't a "normal," 3-D relationship. It's something far beyond that. And if you're only seeking Union, you may be missing the point. Union does happen for many, and others are still seeking it.

But one thing I've learned on my Journey is that what is perhaps more important than the Journey to Union with your Beloved, Your Twin Flame, is the Journey to self-understanding and unconditional self-love.

In our 3-D world, the focus is on romantic connections, living happily ever after, getting married, having kids, and staying together forever. It is the centerpiece of virtually every Disney movie. While all of it is awesome, these are all 3-D constructs.

This relationship is NOT about all of that. It is (probably) far more than our minds can even comprehend. It is about a perfect, unconditional love in the 5-D (to be brought "down" into the 3-D), a love that is **not** rooted in fear, possession, manipulation, or control. It is the purest form of love. Love without expectations, without conditions. A love like Isis had for Osiris. A love like Jesus had for Mary Magdalene. A love like Clare of Assisi had for St. Francis. A love to surpass all loves.

Through this love, you will be brought to your knees and you will rise to the highest of highs. Through it all, you will learn about your vulnerabilities and insecurities, and those "shadow" aspects of your Self, as well as your core wounds, that need to be healed.

Everything will rise to the surface along the Journey to be noticed, purged, and healed. Nothing will remain hidden. The purging which happens (and is necessary) on both sides and the healing bring both of the Twins to a closer state of purity and in alignment not only with one another, but perhaps more important, the Divine. Once the Twins are aligned with one another and the Divine, they are free and unfettered to work on their combined Soul Purpose/Soul Mission.

Of course, the Twins can work on their Soul Purpose/ Soul Mission whether they are romantically "together" or not. If you are so focused on Union, but you have not yet healed your shadow self or core wounds, then it would not be possible to enter into Union with your Beloved for long, if at all. Your approach must be balanced and it must be somewhat detached from a specific outcome. You can hope, you can pray.

Stay positive, but just remember, this is an evolving process. Truly, as my guides have shared with me, "It's a *'daily unfolding.'*" Stay true to your intuition and to your own heart. Stay faithful. Always act out of love. Do what you think is right.

There may be a time or times when you choose to walk away from the Journey, and that is okay, too. That, too, will then become part of your Journey. The Twins are like a magnet and it may not be long before you are drawn back to one another. And that is okay, too. Stick with the "daily unfolding." Don't lose heart, and don't lose hope. Look at your progress regularly, look at how far you've come since the beginning, and be proud of that. You've come a long, long way on your Journey, there's a reason for it, and it "ain't over until it's over" (channeling Lenny Kravitz).

Why I Still Believe

I been in a cave
For forty days
Only a spark
To light my way

I wanna give out
I wanna give in
This is our crime
This is our sin

But I still believe
I still believe
Through the pain
And through the grief

Through the lies
Through the storms
Through the cries
And through the wars

Oh, I still believe

Flat on my back
Out at sea
Hopin' these waves
Don't cover me

I'm turned and tossed
Upon the waves
When the darkness comes
I feel the grave

But I still believe
I still believe
Through the cold
And through the heat

Through the rain
And through the tears
Through the crowds
And through the cheers

Oh, I still believe

I'll march this road
I'll climb this hill
Upon my knees
If I have to

I'll take my place
Upon this stage
I'll wait till the end of time
For you like everybody else

I'm out on my own
Walkin' the streets
Look at the faces
That I meet

I feel like I
Like I wanna go home
What do I feel?
What do I know?

But I still believe
Yes, I still believe
Through the shame
And through the grief

Through the heartache
Through the tears
Through the waiting
Through the years

For people like us
In places like this
We need all the hope
That we can get

Oh, I still believe

-"I Still Believe," by Tim Capello, Lost Boys Movie Soundtrack (1987)

Why do I still believe in this Journey, even though my Twin Flame and I are not in Union yet and I have no tangible results in the "real world" of that which I've sought? This is an important question to answer. The Twin Flame Journey is a Journey of faith and the truth is, it may never be finished. Abraham Hicks says the work is never finished; it can never be completely done.

The greatest thing that first comes to my mind is that this Journey came to me from the ether, like a dream, but more like a miracle. The fact that I had this dream that shook me out of the slumber of my ordinary life and jerked me up by my collar, and made me see life, love, relationships, unconditional love (and in fact, everything) in new ways I had never even conceived before, well, that's a miracle in and of itself. That is 100%, bonafide, supernatural shit. (Pardon the expression, but it's true.)

Through the Journey, though it was scary and nerve-wracking at times, I was able to correct the dynamics between me and my karmic partner. I was able to put proper distance between her and me. I was able to establish healthier boundaries with her. I was able to demand more respect from her. We are now able to co-parent our children with minimum disruption and we did this through the day-to-day (gentle) sharing of hard truths and expression of wants and needs. Together, but apart.

I can compare the fresh, new feeling I have to seeing the world for the first time and seeing possibilities like a small child because you have no set expectations and you haven't learned to want or to fear. Truly, it was like being re-born. Just when I thought that there was nothing new to see or feel or touch or hear or taste. The Journey opened my eyes up to every possibility, the beauty of a butterfly, the quiet soul of a tree, the sacredness of the ground in which I dig my bare toes, the spiritual gifts that I had always known were there, but didn't know how to articulate or tap into. The Journey meant I could wake in the morning with hope and love on my heart, and that I would carry that in me throughout the day and into the evening, every day.

If you take Union out of the equation and it (the relationship, the joining) never transpires in the 3-D, in the real world, then that is okay, too. Complete and total surrender means you can accept that, because you know that the Heavens have something even greater in mind for you. Along this Journey, you learn to trust the process, your guides, and the Creator/Universe/Source Energy. That energy, that power, which always has your back, never lies to you and never misleads you. You've just got to let go and trust, again and again and again. That is our pledge, and that is our test.

And to be honest, it's okay that I am writing this book when I am not in physical Union with my Twin, and that's because, through the process, she and I have already come into alignment and into Union together. We share telepathy, we can be together in the 5-D, she is always in my heart and on my mind during virtually every minute of every day. I know what she would say in any given instance, and she knows me, too. When I need energy and positivity, she sends it. When she needs it, I know it and I send it right back. We are now operating as one, in a Union I could never have imagined before. And that's something.

Thank you for coming with me on this Journey. I wish you well. I wish you love. I wish you unconditional love that surpasses all human understanding. And with that, I'll leave you with this quote from the love-master, Rumi:

*"Lovers don't finally meet somewhere. **They're in each other all along**." –* **Rumi**

Appendix

K.D. Courage's Playlist: Twin Flame Songs to Get You Through

If you're like me, music is a big part of your life. It's a big part of my personal coping mechanism. Like since I was born. I've found that really good music can help you keep your vibration high when you are feeling low on your Journey. I've developed/devised just the playlist to keep you sane and feeling that unconditional love vibe, but, a word of warning: I am a child of the 70s and 80s, so my playlist reflects that decade, plus many of the ones that followed. This list resonates with me and my Journey and may not be for you. Please feel free to send me your fave songs for the Journey (and we'll keep on updating this list).

- "Miracles," by Jefferson Starship
- "Send Her My Love," by Journey
- "Gold," by Spandau Ballet
- "Broken Wings," by Mister Mister
- "Sweet Freedom," by Michael McDonald

- "Piano in the Dark," by Brenda Russell
- "Promises, Promises," by Naked Eyes
- "Two Occasions," by Babyface
- "I'd Die Without You," by P.M. Dawn
- "I Knew You Were Waiting," by Aretha Franklin and George Michael
- "Almost Love," by Sabrina Carpenter
- "Damn, I Wish I Was Your Lover," by Sophie B. Hawkins
- "No Ordinary Love," by Sade
- "How Can I Fall," by Breathe
- "Seven Wonders," by Fleetwood Mac
- "Sara," by Fleetwood Mac
- "Something About You," by Level 42
- "Hands to Heaven," by Breathe
- "Live to Tell," by Madonna
- "Make it Last Forever," by Keith Sweat
- "Come Back to Me," by Janet Jackson
- "Heart and Soul," by T'Pau
- "Alive and Kicking," by Simple Minds
- "Hard to Say I'm Sorry," by Chicago
- "Miss You All the Time," by O.A.R.
- "If You Were Here," by the Thompson Twins
- "We Belong Together," by Mariah Carey
- "Crazy for You," by Madonna

- "Against All Odds," by Phil Collins
- "Sara," by Starship
- "I Belong to You," by Lenny Kravitz
- "It Ain't Over 'til It's Over," by Lenny Kravitz
- "One Headlight," by the Wallflowers
- "Eyes Without a Face," by Billy Idol
- "Vision of Love," by Mariah Carey
- "One More Try," by George Michael
- "Waiting in Vain," by Annie Lennox
- "Kissing a Fool," by George Michael
- "What You Won't Do for Love," by Bobby Caldwell
- "Feeling Good," by Michael Buble
- "This is It," by Kenny Loggins
- "Biggest Part of Me," by Ambrosia
- "Breathe Again," by Toni Braxton
- "Your Song," by Rita Ora
- "I Will Possess Your Heart," by Death Cab for Cutie
- "#41," by Dave Matthews Band
- "The Difficult Kind," by Sheryl Crow
- "Building a Mystery," by Sarah McLachlan
- "Just Another Day," by Jon Secada
- "Head Over Heels," by Tears for Fear
- "Don't You (Forget About Me)," by Simple Minds

- "Tender Love," by Force MD's
- "Never Tear Us Apart," by INXS
- "Twist of Fate," by Olivia Newton John
- "Wait by the River," by Lord Huron
- "Beloved," by Mumford & Sons
- "Trouble," by Lindsey Buckingham
- "Trouble," by Shawn Colvin
- "Big Love," by Fleetwood Mac
- "Old Love," by Eric Clapton
- "Sit Next to Me," by Foster the People
- "Higher Love," by Steve Winwood
- "I Get Weak," by Belinda Carlisle
- "I Feel it Comin'," by The Weeknd, Featuring Daft Punk
- "A Different Corner," by George Michael
- "Sunflower," by Post Malone and Swae Lee
- "Give Me Some Kind of Sign Girl," by Brenton Wood
- "Beyond," by Leon Bridges
- "You're the Only Woman," by Ambrosia
- "Kiss From a Rose," by Seal
- "So Into You," by Atlanta Rhythm Section
- "Sign Your Name," by Terence Trent D'Arby
- "A Million Dreams" (From the Greatest Showman), by Pink

- "Wide Awake," by Katy Perry
- "Close to You," by Maxi Priest
- "Young Turks," by Rod Stewart
- "Dark Side," by Kelly Clarkson
- "Sacred Love," by Bad Brains
- "Ain't Nobody," by Chaka Khan
- "Cruel Summer," by Bananarama
- "Fake Love," by Drake
- "Broken," by Lovelytheband
- "Alone Again Or," by The Damned
- "Don't Dream It's Over," by Crowded House
- "Bleed to Love Her," by Fleetwood Mac
- "I Love You," by the Climax Blues Band
- "Automatic," by The Pointer Sisters
- "The Beautiful Ones," by Prince
- "I Can Dream About You," by Dan Hartman
- "Walk Me Home," by Pink
- "Suddenly Last Summer," by The Motels
- "Only the Lonely," by The Motels
- "Like to Get to Know You Well," by Howard Jones
- "What is Love," by Howard Jones
- "No One is to Blame," by Howard Jones
- "Two Hearts Beat as One," by U2
- "Is This Love," by Whitesnake

- "Headed for a Heartbreak," by Winger
- "Movement," by Hozier
- "Ascension," by Maxwell
- "Cover Me," by Bruce Springsteen
- "Tunnel of Love," by Bruce Springsteen
- "Confusion," by New Order
- "Girl Can't Help It," by Journey
- "Every Time You Go Away," by Paul Young
- "Mad About You," by Belinda Carlisle
- "Love Hangover," by Donna Summer
- "Need You Now," by Lady Antebellum
- "Two Hearts Beat as One," by U2
- "Captain of Her Heart," by Double
- "Message of Love," by the Pretenders
- "Good Things Fall Apart," by Illenium/Jon Bellion

K.D. Courage's "Watch Later" List: Twin Flame Movies to Help You on Your Way

Just like there are many songs that can help you along your Journey, there are also many movies that are similar to, or indirectly about, the Twin Flame experience. While the following list is not by any means exhaustive, it gives you a good starting point. Sometimes, when we're feeling down about this Journey, it helps to watch a movie that captures and reflects true unconditional love and the many obstacles along the way, and how the leading heroes and heroines handle the challenges of their Journeys.

Like the musical playlist, feel free to send me additional movies that you think should have made this list (and thank you in advance!):

- Titanic (1997)
- Casablanca (1942)
- The Notebook (2004)
- Two of a Kind (1983)
- The Lake House (2006)
- Eternal Sunshine of the Spotless Mind (2004)
- Love in the Time of Cholera (2007)

- Ghost (1990)
- The Princess Bride (1987)
- Sleepless in Seattle (1993)
- You've Got Mail (1998)
- Romeo & Juliet (1996; also 2013)
- Kate & Leopold (2001)
- City of Angels (1998)
- The Fountain (2006)
- Notting Hill (1999)
- Serendipity (2001)
- I Remember You (2015)
- Legends of the Fall (1994)
- I Origins (2014)
- In Your Eyes (2014)
- Fallen (2016)
- Tristan & Isolde (2006)
- Midnight Bayou (2009)
- Till Human Voices Wake Us (2002)
- 2:22 (2017)
- Somewhere in Time (1980)
- Café de Flore (2011)
- Loving (2016)
- Like Water for Chocolate (1992)
- Made in Heaven (1987)
- After (2012)

- Upside Down (2012)
- Beyond Borders (2004)
- Pride & Prejudice (2005)
- Sense & Sensibility (1995)
- Bridget Jones' Diary Trilogy (2001-2016)
- Frequencies (2014)
- Only You (1994)
- Your Name (2016)
- Endless Love (2014)
- A Star is Born (2018)
- 500 Days of Summer (2009)
- What Dreams May Come (1998)
- Infinity (1996)
- One Day (2011)
- If Only (2004)
- Comet (2014)

Some Questions and Answers About the Twin Flame Journey

Does the Journey make you question everything you thought love was, even though you are married?

Yes. Before your Journey, you will think you know and understand love in its various forms. During the Journey, you will realize how limiting your beliefs about love were. You will see how you were keeping love contained, in a box, with every limitation and restriction and condition on it imaginable. During the Journey, your heart opens up and you realize you have more room in your heart for love, that you can love more than one person, that you can love unconditionally, and that you can love EVERYONE unconditionally. That is the beauty of the Journey.

Many people are in prior commitments and marriages when they meet their Twin in the real world, or in the 3-D. Some people are able to work through this in their marriages, while others wrestle with it for many years. Some will leave their marriages. It really depends on the couple and the situation, as well as the person. One of the important things to remember: Try to always act with integrity and try to always "do it clean," meaning: Treat your partner with the same respect you would want to be treated. Honor yourself and your partner. Try to tell your authentic truth as often and as much as you can. It will be very difficult on both you and your partner/spouse, but it is necessary. The working through of issues with your partner or spouse is also part of your Journey.

How many people are unhappy with their spouse or partner but do not articulate it because it's too difficult? Or because you don't want to hurt him or her? How does that serve you? How does that serve him or her? What would happen if you were more honest? Could you get more out of your relationship? Could you get more out of life? Could you get more of the things that you actually want?

In my case, honesty has solved a lot of issues in all of my relationships. Through the Journey, I have learned to be more transparent and authentic. As I always say, though, this Journey is not for the faint of heart. Try to honor what is best and most true about yourself. Just know that your capacity to love, to truly LOVE, is infinite, and that is nothing of which to feel ashamed. It just is.

How can you reach your Twin in his/her thoughts or dreams?

Connecting in the fifth dimension is a way you can tap into your Twin Flame's thoughts and dreams.

You may ask yourself whether telepathy with your Twin is really possible or if it is really happening. Have no doubt. It is. This has been confirmed by many Twins. When you become frustrated because of no communication in the 3-D, it's important to remember, you can talk to your Twin anytime, telepathically. How do you do this, you ask? It's simple. It's as simple as talking to your friend or your mother or a family member.

1) Think of your Beloved anytime. Or you can do this before bedtime, as well, to "meet up" in the dreamspace.

2) Set the intention that you want to communicate telepathically with your Twin or that you want to have dreams of him or her. You can say something as simple as, "I intend to..." or "I set my intention to communicate in the 5-D with [NAME]." Or, "I intend to dream about my Twin." Or even a request, if you are so inclined, a prayer. You can pray and ask for connection with your Twin in thoughts or dreams.

3) Then, in the immortal words of John Mayer, "Say what you need to say." I've communicated short phrases up to the contents of entire letters to my Twin during the daytime and in the evenings, too.

This communication is bi-directional and can help you continue to remain close to your Twin. It can allow you to convey important things you need to say, even when you are in Separation. The best part? You can do this anytime. You'll soon start to see (or hear) proof from your Twin that this is working, or you may start to see progress in your Twin Flame Journey.

Just try it. Curious to see if it works for you. It has for me. Good luck!

How do I overcome the regrets of how strange I behaved, conducted myself, and feeling I pushed away my Twin Flame away from me during the Separation phase?

The Twin Flame Journey is not for the faint of heart. On both sides, both parties can—and do—behave strangely. First of all, the Journey knocks you off balance, and can turn your world upside down. An ordinarily confident person can find themselves suddenly a jabbering and needy idiot. A normally composed person may suddenly lash out at someone for no apparent reason.

If you flee, you may do so because you are confused or overcome with emotion. This Journey is most likely not like anything you've ever experienced before. As humans, we try to categorize experiences and relationships into tidy, neat little boxes. A Twin Flame "relationship" cannot be neatly fit into any category. There is no prior "memory file" with which to compare the intense emotions and feeling of the connection.

You will feel the love is too intense, too much. You may find the "relationship" or the constant thoughts of your Twin too distracting. It may distract you from your normal duties or responsibilities.

The bottom line: Please, forgive yourself if you acted strangely, conducted yourself in ways you wouldn't normally. Please also forgive yourself if you pushed your Twin away, over and over again. You didn't know what you didn't know. Neither party will understand it right away. Confusion breeds fear. Fear breeds...well, behavior you may not be proud of.

Just know this: Your Twin, if he/she is a true Twin, will forgive you, because the Journey is about unconditional love. He or she will realize that you were running from the intensity of the connection. He or she will understand you may run because there were parts of yourself, or parts of your experience, that you just weren't ready to deal with yet. And it's all okay. It's all part of the process. Those feelings of regret are usually felt on both sides. Just know your Twin probably has some regrets, too. In divine timing, it will all work out.

What if the Twin Flame Journey is not real? My runner admits no love (beyond friendship) for me yet his behavior reveals differently. How do I keep believing?

This is a question that many on the Journey grapple with and those who are not on the Journey will not understand. I think you must trust your intuition as it usually does not lead us wrong.

However, with that said, it is important to respect people's boundaries and they may not see things as you do (even though they may be projecting a certain behavior)...their words may be very different than their actions. This could be part of the ego/mask that one Twin wears to spur self-realization and self-growth in the other Twin. The 3-D answer is, "[He] or [She] is not interested. Move on." The Twin Flame Journey answer is: The 3-D projection of him or her is projecting that which triggers in you a response which spurs your own self-growth and soul development (if you are not on the Journey, you may not understand this.) This triggering will continue (on both sides) until your inner wounds are acknowledged, addressed, and healed.

If you go into a period of Separation, you will continue to communicate in other ways: In the dreamspace and through telepathy. If you are a true Twin on a true Journey, you will see signs, synchs, miracles, and manifestations that illustrate to you, that your Journey is indeed, a real and tangible thing.

The goal is not to keep believing. The goal is to keep searching, healing, and addressing the inner parts of yourself that are standing in your own way. Sometimes it takes the Journey to unearth these aspects. The ultimate goal is to come into acceptance and love of your own Self. This is the point of the Journey. If you are lucky, too, Union with your Person may happen in this lifetime. Just keep believing and keep going. Stay optimistic. Believe in possibilities. Try to stay positive. If your person needs space, certainly give it to him or her. You cannot force anyone into anything they do not feel led or drawn to do. If you are true Twins, things will come together in beautiful ways. It is, above all, a Journey of Faith.

How do I keep from hurting so much while my Twin Flame and I are not talking? She is the runner and I am the chaser. She asked me almost a month ago to not contact her anymore and I haven't, but it feels like my soul is missing.

Goodness, I feel your pain and know it all too well. This is really tough on the Journey because, on the one hand, you're feeling all these extremely intense emotions and a connection you cannot explain, and perhaps on the other hand, someone is telling you that they don't feel the connection, too, or that they're "just not that into you." Or to please leave them alone and then perhaps they block you on social media or don't return messages. It hurts, like the deepest hurt you can imagine. You follow your intuition, just as you always have, and yet, it seems it has betrayed you.

Most likely, it has not. And your runner will run from the connection for possibly many reasons.

It's important to look at a few things related to why chasers chase, and why runners run.

I believe we, as so-called, "chasers" or Divine Feminines, chase our Twin, our Divine Counterpart, because we are so acclimated to the typical 3-D approach to love and relationships. To obtain love, we believe we must court it, we must follow our emotions to their natural equivalent of actions to cement the connection, to try to "make it real." We then try to "wrestle it to the ground." But on the Twin Flame Journey, things don't work as they do in the 3-D, and your usual methods that work so well to attract someone to you and to keep them there, don't work at all, much to your dismay.

Many of us may be desperate for love and affection and an authentic connection, and when we think we sense it, we run toward it with all our energy and all our might. We will do practically anything to try to make it real (at least, as real as it is in our own hearts and minds.)

I believe we chase because we may not be fully confident in our own skins. We do not love ourselves in a sufficient way, and so we are always seeking love from somewhere outside of us, just like we are always seeking validation outside of us. We don't yet know that true love and true acceptance starts with ourselves, and we must love ourselves wholly and completely first before anyone else can—or will. We must feel whole inside of ourselves before we can join with another.

I also sense that we chase on the Journey (time and again) to keep it feeling "real." We want our Twin Flame to acknowledge the connection, to admit they feel the same way that we do. We feel we must accomplish this above all else (again, as proof of the connection). When this doesn't happen, it can trigger us and send us into spirals of self-doubt, sadness, and even depression.

Divine Masculines are "typically" the runner though the roles can at times switch, as I have come to understand it. I am not a Divine Masculine, but I will do my best to address why Divine Masculines run, as I understand it, from everything I have personally experienced and everything I have read and heard on the Journey. Many, including those who self-identify as Divine Masculines, say they run because the Twin Flame connection is too intense. It brings up too much in their emotional field: too much doubt, too many questions. Also, they feel they're not ready for such a "big love." They're not ready to experience such intense emotions and the deep spiritual connection. In fact, some of them may not be ready for any type of real love, or authentic love. He or she may have gotten used to the 3-D templates of love and sex and that is all they have learned to expect. A new experience, or the potential of a new experience, perhaps "blows their minds" and they don't know what to do with it.

They may also run because of certain 3-D realities, such as when the other Twin has a partner, a spouse, kids, a family. It may be too messy or inconvenient to disrupt (or seemingly disrupt) a family unit that is on the outside, by all accounts, a "happy family."

There can also be family issues on the part of the Divine Masculine that he or she must face, like perhaps the concern that relationship won't be accepted by their own family because of things like the gender, race, or socioeconomic status of their Twin, or the age difference between him or her and the Twin.

Another key factor of why Divine Masculines run is because they may associate the karma and karmic lessons that come as a result of the Journey, with the Divine Feminine. It may appear to them that she caused it all, or that she is at fault, or that she did something to bring all of this upon the both of them when, in fact, it is a collaborative Journey and a collaborative, co-creative "project" between the two Twins for the benefit of both of them. This co-creation is designed so that both souls can experience these karmic lessons and process through them so that they can both resolve issues and achieve true soul growth.

In fact, some Twins may experience all of the above. These obstacles, while huge, are not insurmountable, as many Twins in Union can attest. Sometimes it requires a miracle, or many miracles, but if you're like me, you believe in miracles. You've seen them firsthand. This Journey is no different.

The truth is, you CAN still remain connected and communicate using telepathy and when you are in the dream state. It is highly possible your Twin is coming through in your dreams and giving you messages. As always, trust your intuition. Also, if she asks you to back off in the 3-D (a.k.a. "Real World"), you should do so and respect her wishes, but if a good deal of time passes and you feel compelled to reach out again, check your "gut" but always go with your heart. Be prepared to be rejected possibly time and again. It will trigger in you the things that need to be healed and is necessary for your soul growth and development.

Remember, this is a Journey that you both have CO-CREATED. Through the rejection, we can slough off past hurts and core wounding related to rejection, abandonment, feeling unloved, and self-worth issues.

Through this Journey, if you learn to process through all of that, you'll be in a much better state and vibrational match to attract your Twin. The hurt will ebb and flow, but when you do the work, you will improve in ways you never thought possible. And you will be grateful for all the Journey brought you, the extreme highs, and even the lows. Trust me on this. It will happen. Just do your work, breathe, and relax. What is meant to happen will happen, all in Divine Timing.

What do you do if your Twin Flame rejects you?

When your Twin Flame rejects you, that is part of the process. It is designed to trigger in you that which needs to be acknowledged, cleared, and healed. You should let your feelings flow in and flow out, but do not let them "stick with you." Feel the feelings, but then use your healing mode of preference (prayer, meditation, talking it out with a friend, etc.) to transmute the "negative" emotions. These emotions could be fear of abandonment, fear of rejection, fear of being alone, or fear of the connection not "succeeding" or coming to fruition. It can also trigger feelings of hopelessness and loss. These are all natural emotions and are very much normal to the process. But in order to ascend, we must clear out these emotions in our energy fields so that we can be lighter and brighter. In this way, we are able to evolve and ascend into a better state of being.

Please Note: This process may need to be repeated over and over again. Each time, the feelings should grow less intense and less troublesome.

There are many great guided meditations on YouTube for the clearing of "negative" emotions. You can find guided meditations for virtually any feeling/situation. I would look for those videos that have a high number of followers and a high number of "likes."

Has speaking to other Twin Flames created more doubt, confusion and negativity in your own Journey?

No. Speaking with other Twin Flames has only strengthened my belief in Twin Flames and around it. It has minimized confusion and created more positivity. One of the most important things you can do for yourself on this Journey is to find like-minded souls who align with you and your beliefs, who are positive and a good influence and who you can trust and confide in.

With that said, there are SOME online Twin Flame groups that are not positive and not high energy. You can read and feel the toxic feelings and energy expressed on some of these platforms. I would suggest if it doesn't feel good or right to you, move on to another group that feels better. After all, this Journey is about personal Soul Growth and mastery. Once you level up, different people will resonate with you. Aim for the higher frequencies. Be realistic with your expectations, though. Soul Growth and development takes time. Be gentle with yourself. Be gentle with your Twin. Remember: This is a co-creative process between you and your Twin designed for both of your growth and development.

Reviews

If you enjoyed this book or found it helpful along your Journey, please leave a positive review on Amazon or wherever (or however) you're reading this.

If you have suggestions for improvement or other feedback, please share that privately with me at twinflameguidebook@gmail.com so that your feedback can be included in a future review of this book, and in future editions. If you have less than constructive criticism, I ask that you please share that elsewhere. I appreciate your understanding and I thank all of us for collectively going on this Journey.

About the Author

K.D. Courage is a Twin Flame who has been on the journey for many years. A former corporate executive who started her career in publishing, K.D. now focuses her attention on using her gifts (spiritual and otherwise) to help men and women achieve a lighter, brighter, and better state of being. K.D. is a certified Reiki healer and has also authored pieces in books, websites, magazines, newspapers, newsweeklies, and literary magazines. In her spare time (when she's not writing), she's spending time with her family, creating art, doing photography, bicycling, swimming, and working on reviving her musical aspirations (always a work in progress). K.D. has worked with more than 40 non-profits and not-for-profits, serving on the boards of several of them and providing them with time, resources, funding, and space to help them support their missions. K.D.'s soul purpose is not only "purity" but "to become the perfect vessel for perfect love." While that sounds like a lofty goal, she believes it's 100% achievable.

·

Made in the USA
Middletown, DE
12 December 2020